WHO'S IN CHARGE?

ALSO BY

Richard M. Clurman

◆

Beyond Malice

To the End of Time

the chief executive press

WHO'S IN CHARGE?

RICHARD M. CLURMAN

whittle direct books

Photographs: Robert C. Stempel by Patrick Harbron/Sygma, page 11;
John F. Smith by Michael L. Abramson, page 11; Ira M. Millstein by Stan
Godlewski, page 11; John F. Akers by Robert Deutsch, *USA Today*, page 17;
James D. Robinson by John Abbott, page 21; Paul E. Lego by Roger Mas-
troianni, page 21; Dale Hanson by Robert Holmgren, page 39;
Richard C. Breeden by David Burnett/Contact Press Images, page 46;
Kenneth A. Macke by Layne Kennedy, page 61.

The Chief Executive Press: Dorothy Foltz-Gray, Senior Editor;
Ken Smith, Design Director; Evelyn Ellis, Art Director

Library of Congress Catalog Card Number: 93-060382
Clurman, Richard M.
Who's in Charge?
ISBN 1-879736-15-2
ISSN 1060-8923

the chief executive press

The Chief Executive Press presents original short books by distinguished authors on subjects of special importance to the topmost executives of the world's major businesses.

The series is edited and published by Whittle Books, a business unit of Whittle Communications L.P. Books appear several times a year, and the series reflects a broad spectrum of responsible opinions. In each book the opinions expressed are those of the author, not the publisher or the advertiser.

I welcome your comments on this ambitious endeavor.

William S. Rukeyser
Editor in Chief

CONTENTS

PREFACE

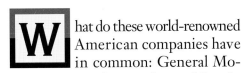**W**hat do these world-renowned American companies have in common: General Motors, American Express, IBM, Westinghouse, Sears, Macy's, Digital Equipment, Goodyear, Tenneco, Kodak, Chrysler, and Polaroid?

Astonishingly, despite their lustrous pasts, all have been under siege by their boards of directors or shareholders in the two years since 1991. All have been forced either to replace their chief executive officers (GM, AmEx, IBM, Westinghouse, Macy's, Digital, Goodyear, Tenneco, Chrysler) or to reorganize (Sears, Kodak, Polaroid). None of the upheavals took place quietly. Many other companies shared their fate.

Page-one headlines blared to the world the news of repeated traumas at the heart of the American enterprise system. "Creative destruction," economist Joseph A. Schumpeter had labeled these once rare business uproars decades earlier. Suddenly they have become commonplace.

In one week in early 1993, the boards and shareholders of three corporate titans blasted their CEOs from their thrones. It was the fastest and biggest shootout at the highest ranks of business power in all of American history. Similar explosions had dislodged dozens of other chief executive officers the year before.

In the '80s, CEOs worried about takeovers from the outside. Now they needed to worry about takeovers from inside.

"All you have to do is note the stories of the 52-year-old executives who for reasons of health, for personal reasons, or increasingly at the request of the board, are departing almost daily," said H. Brewster "Bruce" Atwater Jr., CEO of General Mills and chairman of the Business Roundtable's Corporate Governance Task Force. "It used to be treated with politesse and oblique language. Now it's out in the open."

What's going on? Whatever happened to those cozy old relationships—the men's club of board members nurtured and dominated by the CEOs who picked them? What forged shareholders into such a potent force when they were once so widely dispersed and helpless ("little old ladies in tennis shoes," "Aunt Minnies and Uncle Earls")?

Shareholders were always the owners of public companies. But in another era they quietly sold their stock and bought another if they were dissatisfied with their investment. "The Wall Street Walk," the sedate waltz was called.

No longer. Today shareholder complaints are a noisy rock and roll amplified by the media around a bandstand labeled "corporate governance."

Former New York comptroller Edward V. Regan, who in 1993 gave up his 14-year trusteeship of the state's $56 billion employee retirement fund, explained the new cacophony: "Boards of directors are finally waking up to the fact that many investors want more than to just buy shares on good news and sell on bad." Rawleigh Warner Jr., onetime chairman and CEO of Mobil and now a blue-chip director who has served on many other boards, including AmEx, Time, and Chemical Bank, personifies the shift. Weeks before he led the coup to oust AmEx CEO James D. Robinson III, Warner said, "Much as I never wanted to be a cat among the pigeons, I now feel I have to when things aren't going well." Added former Avon chairman Hicks B. Waldron, who sits on four boards (Atlantic Richfield, Hilton Hotels, Ryder System, and CIGNA), "No one is happy to say we fired the bastard. It doesn't do the company any good." Increasingly, directors clench their teeth and fire him anyway.

William S. Rukeyser, the managing editor of *Money* and *For-*

tune magazines in the '70s and '80s, remembered, "When I heard the term *corporate governance* back then, I thought mostly of Ralph Nader and South African divestiture advocates." John Pound, a Harvard finance professor and an adviser to business and shareholder groups, wrote, "Taken in sum, the record of 1992 suggests a revolution in American corporate governance."

John L. Grant, a director of Air Products & Chemicals, a producer of specialty gases based in Allentown, Pennsylvania, drew the same conclusion. In a 1992 *Wall Street Journal* article titled "Shield Outside Directors From Inside Seduction," he wrote, "Corporate governance is a hot topic these days, inflamed by the lethargic response of boards to underperformance by corporate managements. The same questions always emerge: 'What are the directors doing? Are they asleep? Are they in management's pocket?'"

How does a CEO protect himself and his management in this new atmosphere?

What are directors' new responsibilities and the role of the board?

What have shareholders a right to demand?

Do CEOs, directors, and shareholders need their own "new covenant"?

When I started to explore these questions in 1992, I was often asked—as writers and journalists always are—What are you working on? At first I confidently replied, Corporate governance. Eh? What's that? Shorthand lingo, I explained, for who's in charge of a public company: the CEO, the board, or the shareholders. It still sounded like a sleepy subject. A year later it looked more like a nightmare for the CEOs and directors of many landmark American companies.

Everyone in the U.S. is concerned about the economy. "It's the economy, stupid" was the marching order that won the 1992 presidential election. Yet surprising as it may seem to people involved in the affairs of big business, their hot-button term of the '90s, corporate governance, is as unfamiliar outside their world as astronomical thermodynamics might be to most people worried about global warming.

At President Clinton's preinaugural economic summit, more than 300 business executives, economists, and analysts discussed

America's urgent economic problems for two days without ever using the words *corporate governance*. The phrase is never mentioned on the hustings by politicians, nor is it recognizable in the vocabulary of most Americans' everyday lives. No wonder the public doesn't understand the term. "Corporate governance," said a specialist on the subject, "is one of the great mysteries of the business world." Yet in the precincts of business power it has become a byword.

The tension, one financial reporter moaned, "could spoil a lot of executive breakfasts across the country" unless CEOs and their directors pay attention.

They are paying attention.

In some instances, too much attention.

Library bookshelves strain under the weight of thousands of books, monographs, statistical studies, charts, and learned research papers on the subject. Dozens of newsletters and specialized periodicals for CEOs, directors, and shareholders flood the mails tracking the latest news and ponderings. The newest offering in the crowded field, the bimonthly *Corporate Governance Advisor*, trumpeted its birthright in the maiden issue: "The current interest in corporate governance is a reflection of the widespread belief that our country's economic prowess is in decline and that the ground rules in the corporate enterprise are partly responsible."

Since 1992, more than 50 seminars, discussion groups, and even a public television program have been devoted to corporate governance. Everybody from the chairmen of the Securities and Exchange Commission and the New York Stock Exchange to professional directors, investment fund managers, management consultants, executive recruiters, legal eminences, judges, and CEOs makes speeches and writes papers on it. Study groups convene at leading business and law schools. Scholarly articles fill academic journals. But business school professors "are an anonymous breed, and their research is often denigrated as a blend of big words and small ideas," noted one *New York Times* business reporter.

Corporate governance is Topic A for a new cottage industry made up of trade associations such as the Business Roundtable's Corporate Governance Task Force, the Council of Institutional Investors, Institutional Shareholder Services, United Shareholders Association, and the National Association of Corporate Directors. Since 1990, the computerized information bank Nexis has recorded 3,338 entries under the key words *corporate governance*. The Dow Jones News/Retrieval Service has 2,949.

Is it overkill?

Only if the focus on corporate governance distracts CEOs and boards from the root problems governance is intended to address: global competition, long-term investment and capital formation, jobs, productivity, innovation, research and development, product quality, business-government relations, and social and environmental problems. These tough issues ultimately spell success or failure for the American economy and social system in the '90s.

Corporate governance is only a process. It describes in two words the tangle of relationships among management, boards, and shareholders. It is the structure by which public corporations are monitored. Good governance provides an often rough and heartless means of guarding against failure, but it doesn't guarantee success. Too often business people and their advisers overemphasize the form of the corporation instead of its goals: enhancement of the company's value and reputation.

"Good long-term economic performance is the only meaningful measurement of good corporate governance," said Bruce Atwater, who sits on the boards of General Electric, Merck, and General Mills. In fact, he suggests, companies that concentrate on governance instead of business may do themselves more damage than those less preoccupied.

John F. Welch Jr.'s brutal but financially successful transformation of General Electric included getting rid of more than 170,000 jobs, 117 businesses, and $21 billion in assets. Despite his "Neutron Jack" sobriquet (he kills the people and leaves the buildings standing), Welch remains the most admired CEO in the U.S. according to many of his business peers.

Welch's revolutionary regeneration of GE is detailed in the book *Control Your Own Destiny or Someone Else Will* by GE management consultant Noel M. Tichy and *Fortune* editor Stratford Sherman. In the detailed account of the last 10 years at GE, neither the authors nor Welch ever mentions corporate governance. The role of the board is barely noticed. The book and Welch say only that the board "solidly supported him" and "was absolutely essential." Director G. G. Michelson, a senior vice-president of Macy's and past chairman of the Columbia University Board of Trustees, affirmed that "it was Jack's vision of the future," not the board members or shareholders, that made the difference.

Faulty governance alone is not what brought some of the world's pioneering and preeminent companies to the brink of disaster. The unraveling of IBM, General Motors, American Express, Westinghouse, and others came from clinging to old battle plans in a new worldwide marketplace. In essence, top managers and blue-chip boards allowed their companies to fall from the pinnacle of success. "People like the status quo," said Jack Welch. "They like the way it was. When you start changing things, the good old days look better and better. You've got to be prepared for massive resistance."

These days corporations ignore the question of governance only at their peril. Martin Lipton, the Manhattan lawyer who since the early '70s has dealt with more than 300 companies in crisis, warned those who would avoid the tangled subject: "You're talking about power, the essential power of the nation. When you put it together, it's far more important than political power. What you're dealing with is an attempt to change the power structure. That's why everybody should be interested."

How do busy executives, directors, or shareholder leaders cope with the overload of talk and paper on governance? They are unlikely to plow through the journals or books with titles such as *Small Risk, Stochastic Wealth, and Temporal Assets Return* or *Macro Blueprint: For Dialogue to Shape Tomorrow's Economy*. Many of the analyses, says one business editor, are "written by people who can't write, for people who won't read." Even if they wanted to, business people could not possibly read all the literature or attend the seminars and colloquiums where the subject is earnestly and often profitably addressed.

In his 1992 book *Managing for the Future*, Peter F. Drucker, the management *éminence grise*, reported receiving a letter from an executive asking, "What does [your analysis] mean for me as a senior business executive? What does it mean for my colleagues on the management team? What does it mean for my company? What *action* does it imply—for me, the management team, the company? What opportunities does it identify for us? What changes in goals, strategies, policies, and structure?"

This slim volume is not intended to answer all those questions. But I have attended the conferences, read many of the books, papers, periodicals, newsletters, and monographs, and followed the best and worst cases. Most important, I have interviewed and listened at length to many of the key figures in this ongoing discussion—CEOs, directors, shareholder representatives, academics, and journalists. They offer the voices of live experience. In many cases they provide the pained wisdom of hindsight.

For the most part, I have not presumed to impose my advice on how an up-to-date CEO, an engaged director, or a responsible shareholder should behave. The lessons are here in the evidence. From the experiences of others, some valuable consensus falls into place.

This account attempts to be a reportorial shortcut—a pony edition, if you will, of a 30-volume encyclopedia on corporate governance that has mercifully not yet been published. I draw on a broad array of the experiences, writing, and reporting of others. If the subject matters to you, try this for brevity alone. You may never have time for the immersion others provide.

Why bother? Why should the subject of corporate governance take up your time? Some of the most successful companies have been—and are today—run by entrepreneurs who disdain sharing their governing power. But if you're a CEO or director of a public company, or of a private company thinking about going public, and your business and reputation have been slipping lately—or are just on a plateau—heed the warning of *The Wall Street Journal*: "Two words of advice for laggards in corporate America: start worrying."

But even if—happy days!—your company is doing swimmingly and you are brimming with confidence, start wondering. It could save your job—as well as those of your employees.

Last year, as this series of books was being launched, I reported to you that Cessna Aircraft expected to deliver its 2,000th Citation business jet in early 1993. That aircraft, a stand-up cabin midsize Citation VII, rolled out of our new aircraft completion center in March, and is now in service.

Clearly, 2,000 of anything can be significant only from a relative position. But important to those who will purchase and operate the *next* 2,000 Citations is the worldwide leadership of the Citation fleet, a lead that increases at a greater rate each year. In 1992, Cessna commanded 60 percent of the light and medium business jet market.

About the time the next book in this series reaches you, we will be making final preparations for first flight of the all-new Citation X. Cruising at a remarkable nine-tenths the speed of sound, the Citation X will be the fastest business jet in the world. As our largest and most technologically advanced model, it will be our flagship through the balance of this century.

Our goals are broadly the same as yours: to listen carefully to our customers' needs, and then respond to those needs with efficient and cost-effective products that assist them in achieving and maintaining a competitive edge.

As always, I'd welcome hearing directly from you on any aspect of your business, on this series of CEO books, or with any questions about our company or line of Citations.

Sincerely yours,

Russell W. Meyer, Jr.
Chairman and Chief Executive Officer
Cessna Aircraft Company

Cessna Aircraft Company · One Cessna Boulevard · Wichita, Kansas 67215 · 316/941-7400

Cessna
A Textron Company

Chapter One

APOCALYPSE NOW

In the span of one month late in 1992, a quartet of America's biggest publicly owned companies suffered startling management convulsions. The turmoil at the four was as menacing to other ailing corporations as the seismic rumblings of an approaching earthquake. The site for the noisiest early rumble was the towering General Motors Building on Fifth Avenue in Manhattan, board headquarters for the world's largest industrial company. The 50-story marble-sided slab overlooks Central Park, historic Grand Army Plaza, and the bustling, flag-decked Plaza Hotel—altogether an exalted and tumultuous place for earthshaking events.

Upstairs, on the 25th floor, in the hush of the GM Building, is the company's imposing boardroom. Around its huge burnished table sit the company's 14 directors—the *crème de la crème* of boards. Lest they forget the company's traditional leadership, peering down on them are totemic portraits of every board chairman since GM's founding 85 years ago. H. Ross Perot, a renegade GM director before he was bought out for $750 million, angrily labeled the directors who sat around that table with him "pet rocks who just wanted Lawrence Welk music."

On a late October afternoon, the music playing outside the

grand boardroom was more Wagnerian than Welkian. A purge at the company's highest level was under way. At the storm's epicenter, seven floors above in the offices of Weil, Gotshal & Manges, was Ira M. Millstein, 66, the law firm's best-known partner.

Millstein is a leading apostle of reforming corporate governance, counsel to the outside directors of GM as well as Westinghouse and dozens of other heady companies. For two hours in the conference room adjacent to his office, he philosophized on his favorite subject: how and for whom to run a corporation. He frequently excused himself to take urgent phone calls next door from GM directors and others. Although he won't discuss clients, he was eager to talk about how CEOs, directors, and shareholders should adjust to new realities for the benefit of the economy and the commonweal. "I hate to sound like a missionary," he said between calls, "but I really feel this way. Everybody in the system—management, directors, and shareholders—has to do what he's supposed to do or our system doesn't work."

Millstein knows. The system had not been working well for GM or some of the other companies he advises. GM was losing billions. Its CEO, Robert C. Stempel, a 34-year GM veteran, was on the ropes. The company's stock had plummeted, and its market share was declining. Its labor costs were far out of line, and car quality and design were still suspect. Shareholders and directors were agitated. No display of GM's shiniest models in its chandeliered showroom nor the merriment in F.A.O. Schwarz's toy emporium next door could ease the burden of the CEO and directors who convened upstairs.

Ironically, that day *The Washington Post* broke the news that Stempel, 59, was being forced out after only two years as chairman and CEO. GM spokesmen denied the story. But five days later, after the frenzied phone calls and private meetings, the embattled Stempel resigned. His departure was followed by the resignation from the board of his predecessor, Roger B. Smith.

James Kristie, editor of the quarterly *Directors and Boards*, saw the ouster as a wake-up call for directors: "GM's been the type of company that the institutional investor community feels is a paradigm of a nonperforming company whose board should have stepped in long before this. [The process of firing Stempel] was obviously messier than one might have liked, but it's still a lot closer [to] how we'd like to see boards act."

1988

Declining stock price and market share drove GM's board to oust CEO Robert Stempel (left) in 1992. Counseled by lawyer Ira Millstein (right), the directors named president John Smith (center) chief executive.

◆

At the board meeting a week later, the directors made GM president John F. Smith Jr., 55, the new CEO. Elected as chairman was an outside, independent director, John G. Smale, retired CEO of Procter & Gamble, who had never been an officer of GM. It was the kind of tight collar tailored for many European CEOs but deplored by most American chiefs, who were increasingly forced to share their command.

The shakeup at GM, commented *The New York Times*, "could well turn out to be the shot heard round the corporate world." Ira Millstein declines the huzzahs the press and others gave him for orchestrating the fusillade. "The GM board," he said, "was ready to act. It should have received more credit than it did."

Maybe. But until its 1986 stormy divorce from Ross Perot, GM's board was as ossified as any in America. "Its meetings were mostly ceremonial events," said one director. Millstein's activism in rousing boards and acting as their link to institutional shareholders gave him a much bigger role in the GM revolution than he admits.

Millstein's effectiveness stems in part from his ability to maintain connections with shareholder groups without betraying the boards who retain him. For years he has been giving shareholder leaders hell for concentrating on the wrong things. At a 1987 meeting of the Council on Institutional Investors, he urged shareholders to work with directors and CEOs on company performance, deemphasizing formal governance resolutions.

Dale Hanson is CEO of the powerful $72 billion California Public Employees' Retirement System (Calpers), the largest such pension fund in the U.S. Said Hanson of Millstein: "I think we have a very good working relationship with Ira. He has probably done more [than anyone] to awaken us to what we should focus on—namely the board rather than sins like poison pills. He helped us focus on performance."

Addressing GM's difficulties, Millstein advised directors reluctant to act, while he held off impatient shareholders. Publicly, Millstein catechized that the job of chairman and CEO be split— a heresy given GM's management history. GM's outside directors met privately without the CEO or management directors present, another Millstein recommendation.

One by one a majority of directors were convinced that Stempel had to go and that the new CEO should report to an independent chairman, Millstein's pet remedy for corporate gridlock. "Ira's delivered," said shareholder activist Robert A. G. Monks.

Whether the GM directors were holding a rump meeting at the Marriott Marquis Hotel just off Manhattan's seedy Times Square, conferring in hushed conference telephone calls, or just talking to each other and secretly to the press, outside directors agree that Millstein was an animating presence. He was, said *The Wall Street Journal*, "the chief ideologist of the GM board."

The board's goal became clear, but its performance was ragged to the end. Wrote Paul Ingrassia, Detroit bureau chief for *The Wall Street Journal*: "[Stempel] is out in a messy manner that doesn't reflect particularly well on GM's board. First the directors lay dormant too long. Then they staged an uprising, forcing Mr. Stempel to demote his handpicked president and another key executive. Now they've used newspaper leaks to fire Mr. Stempel before they had to do it themselves." When Ingrassia and Joseph B. White won the 1993 Pulitzer Prize for their GM coverage, Ingrassia acknowledged, "This was a board at the cutting edge of corporate governance activism."

True, GM's board and its attendants were leaking to the press like a gnarled garden hose. One longtime GM director felt it was the press rather than the board that ultimately caused the mess. "I felt no shareholder pressure," he said. "GM did communicate intensively with shareholder groups. But when you're reading a

WHEN WE BUILD MODEL AIRPLANES AT CESSNA, NOBODY GETS GLUE ON THEIR FINGERS.

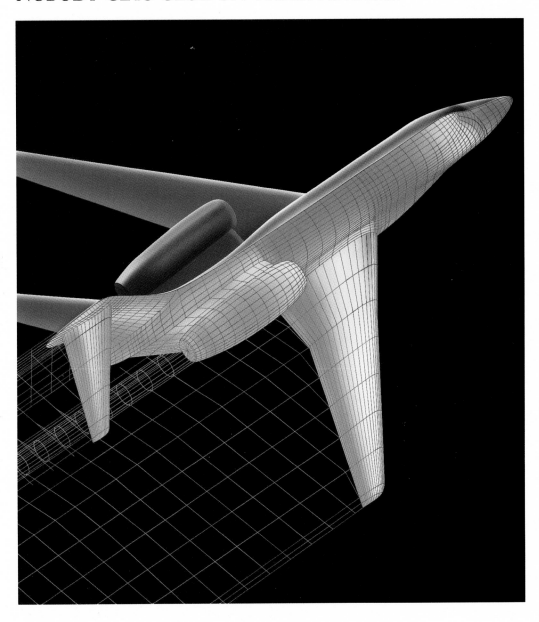

You're looking at a highly advanced computer model of the Citation X. The technology is called Computational Fluid Dynamics (CFD). And it was used to identify areas where airflow would reach transonic and supersonic speeds – allowing engineers to modify the shape of those areas to minimize aerodynamic drag. Before the Citation X, CFD had never been used to measure transonic air speeds on a business jet.

But before the Mach .9 Citation X, it had never really been necessary.

THE SENSIBLE CITATIONS

Cessna
A Textron Company

lot of stuff in the papers about the company and you're getting a lot of activity from these groups, that *does* concern some directors. When the coverage hit, it was hard to handle things differently."

Two weeks later *Fortune* uncovered the second big fault line. This one opened up under the American Express Tower in downtown Manhattan. "The Coup at American Express," read a headline in an advance copy of the biweekly.

Instantly picked up by other news outlets, the word ricocheted around the world in minutes, even before the company could make its formal announcement or the board could pull itself together. According to the company's evasive press release, James D. Robinson III, AmEx's chairman and CEO for close to 16 years, had decided "it was timely to initiate a series of discussions about succession with the board of directors."

Timely indeed. Robinson, the 57-year-old "Teflon CEO," had been under savage attack by some members of his board for months. AmEx had suffered a series of public setbacks. Reports of a tawdry scandal had erupted on the front page of *The Wall Street Journal* (and later in the book *Vendetta* by Bryan Burrough) when AmEx's largest shareholder, international banker Edmond J. Safra, was set up and slandered by a company hit team. Even more painful, AmEx charge cards, the company's trophy business, had fallen on hard times. Compounding Robinson's woes were repeated management storms and financial upheavals following AmEx's acquisition of Shearson Lehman Brothers, the huge investment and brokerage house.

As the company's stock price and earnings fell, Robinson's usually supportive board had little choice. The numbers were unforgiving. AmEx's onetime corporate and civic hero, the model of a patrician U.S. business leader, was on his way out.

In September 1992, Robinson held a predinner meeting at Manhattan's gilded St. Regis Hotel. There he coolly discussed his long-range succession plans and then left the room so that the directors could consider his fate. Rawleigh Warner Jr., the 20-year veteran AmEx director, began the discussion with a lengthy and blistering review of Robinson's past performance. Warner and his allies wanted nothing less than Robinson's departure and a committee of outside directors to pick his replacement. Robinson loyalists were startled and angry. When Robinson rejoined the group for dinner, he and his supporters urged that the process be slowed down.

Instead, Robinson opponents stepped up the pace through secret meetings, caucuses, and lobbying. Three months later, at the end of a five-hour showdown, Robinson's handpicked board decided to compromise, to Wall Street's disappointment. The 19 directors (including nine former and present CEOs of other companies as well as Henry A. Kissinger, Vernon E. Jordan Jr., and Beverly Sills Greenough) made 53-year-old AmEx president Harvey Golub the new CEO, allowing "Gentleman Jim" to keep the chairman's title. AmEx stock dropped 13 percent.

After the stormy arguments, Robinson had maneuvered to hang on as chairman and to take over the Shearson subsidiary. Insiders make up its 16-member board, except for former president Gerald R. Ford and former New York governor Malcolm Wilson. But no face-saving sidesteps could change the conclusion: Robinson was no longer the parent company's boss.

Robinson's biggest ally was AmEx director Drew Lewis, CEO of Union Pacific. "There are [directors] who are maliciously negative about Jim Robinson," Lewis told *New Yorker* writer James B. Stewart. "Take Howard Clark Sr. [AmEx's former CEO] and Rawleigh Warner. They're out to get Harvey [Golub] as an extension of Jim. They're out to scalp him." Robinson got support from other pals, most of whom he had brought on the board. One was Richard M. Furlaud, former president of Bristol-Myers Squibb. Robinson serves on his board and Lewis's as well.

Warner resigned, as did two other dissident directors. "I started the process of urging the board to replace Jimmy," he said. "The board did not see fit to agree. So I didn't feel right, having been so out of line with the rest of the board, about staying on."

The ploy by Robinson and his board backfired. Shareholder representatives instantly descended on the company, complaining that the byzantine new arrangement saved nothing but Robinson's skin. Wall Street and the press hammered AmEx and its board. Four days after the announcement of the new setup, AmEx dropped another bomb. Robinson resigned. The pressure from a dozen major shareholder groups and the press compelled him to leave without even a seat on the board. Robinson had seen what happened at GM and IBM, he said. He and

AmEx were also "likely to continue to be front-page news."

Furlaud, 70, was elected by the board to be the nonexecutive chairman. "Being chairman without being CEO is like being a sprig of parsley on a plate of fish," said a jaundiced executive who had once experienced such an arrangement. The newly elected CEO, Golub, would run the company.

Edmund T. Pratt Jr., director and retired CEO of Pfizer, sits on a number of boards, including Chase Manhattan, International Paper, and, for 17 years, GM. Pratt, whose executive reign lasted for 20 years of rising profits and dividends, sympathizes with less fortunate CEOs. "Poor Jimmy," he said. "He revolutionized AmEx. He made it into a much bigger world factor than it was. When things went well, he was a hero. The more risks you take, as he did, the more chance you have that some fail."

The bruised AmEx board was less sentimental. It did say farewell to Robinson with a million-dollar separation package, including handsome perks and benefits, as well as millions in stock he had accumulated. But the board refused to endow a $750,000 chair at Harvard Business School so that Robinson could teach a course in total quality management; and no, he could not continue to use the corporate jet. Such platinum exit packages, wrote William F. Buckley Jr., a leading conservative and observant Catholic, "give capitalism a bad name, just as hypocritical, fornicating preachers give Christianity a bad name."

Despite necessary involvement, no board wants to handcuff the CEO to day-by-day corporate democracy. After the AmEx board forced Robinson out, it asked Golub to sell Shearson Lehman. Golub quickly offered Shearson to Primerica CEO Sanford I. Weill, who had sold the company to AmEx 12 years before. Most AmEx and Primerica directors knew little about the billion-dollar sale until the CEOs asked for their approval the day after *The Wall Street Journal* reported the sale on page one. Approval was unanimous. Despite their exclusion, no directors or shareholders complained about the swiftness and secrecy of the negotiations.

International Business Machines was the next to hemorrhage in the CEO bloodletting of 1992-93. For half a century "Big Blue" had been the worldwide standard-bearer of American management, quality, and technological magic. Now a mournful chorus

I'm staying, IBM chief John Akers told reporters in December 1992, six weeks before shareholder and board pressure forced him out.

◆

chanted, "The traditional IBM is dead." Grinch-like, IBM chairman and CEO John F. Akers affirmed the ghoulish judgment a week before Christmas. Headed for a $5 billion loss, IBM was having its worst year ever. Akers called for cutbacks that would reduce the company's staff by at least 65,000 in little more than a year, along with billions in budget reductions, including $1 billion from the vaunted research-and-development budget.

Lifetime jobs, an unbroken policy of no layoffs, and some of the best employee benefits in the world were an IBM tradition. Now the company had to transform itself. "[It] has been reduced to a stumbling corporate Cyclops desperately struggling to regain its lost vision," said a *Washington Post* reporter. The conservative columnist George F. Will casually added, "You want the market to punish bad decisions."

The 58-year-old IBM lifer delivered a valiant *mea culpa*. "We have disappointed ourselves and disappointed other people. I feel personal accountability and personal responsibility," Akers explained. But "the board supports me, and I do not plan to step aside." Shareholder groups and journalists were not swayed.

"When John Akers took over as chairman of IBM in 1985, it looked as if he had won the best job in American business," wrote the London *Economist*. "[He] thought that IBM was poised for explosive growth. Instead it has plunged into huge losses, and a chorus of critics is demanding his head."

Dale Hanson, the 50-year-old Pied Piper of unhappy American shareholders and CEO of Calpers, was readying a firing squad for Akers, as were other investment fund leaders. United Shareholders, whose membership includes 400 institutional and 65,000 small investors, loaded four proxy proposals to shoot at Akers at the next annual meeting.

"I met with Akers two months before his announcement," recalled Hanson. "We had a very cordial meeting. He was saying it's going to take a number of years to work things out. I didn't think that was the situation. IBM had some very fundamental problems which required radical surgery." The IBM outside directors, he said, need to do more than "just put their arm around Akers and say, 'He's our guy.'"

Since 1986, Akers had repeatedly reorganized IBM's over-centralized command. But young electronic companies were much spryer than their forebear. "The company's plight," said *The Economist*, "has encouraged many to compare [IBM] to that exemplar of American business myopia, General Motors." The London weekly, along with *Fortune, Business Week* ("IBM's Board Should Clean Out the Corner Office"), and institutional investors all called for Akers's resignation.

Six weeks after Akers and his directors assured the world that he would stay on, the IBM chief resigned. Out with Akers went two of his top executives. "In announcing the sweep at the top," commented *The Wall Street Journal*, "IBM signaled that it, too, had succumbed to the revolution sweeping through corporate America, yielding power to the hands of outside directors." Added one IBM director, "This is a tough board. This is not American Express." A committee of seven of the 14 outside directors started a search for Akers's successor, selecting someone outside the company for the first time in IBM history.

After two months of foraging among prominent CEOs, the search committee picked Louis V. Gerstner Jr., 51, CEO of RJR Nabisco and a former McKinsey consultant and past president of AmEx. Underscoring the need for a radical change in company

FLIES LIKE A JET.
BUYS LIKE A TURBOPROP.

From the moment the first CitationJet took flight, the rules were changed forever. Cruising at 437 mph, the CitationJet is the first business jet that significantly outperforms ordinary turboprops at a guaranteed lower operating cost, *and* costs far less to purchase.

The technological advancements engineered into this extraordinary aircraft mean that even with a smaller price tag, the CitationJet has a great number of things the turboprop does not. Including a bright future.

THE SENSIBLE CITATIONS

Cessna
A Textron Company

culture, IBM's board found a successor to Akers who was a management and dealmaking specialist. He had never worked for a computer company. IBM "needs [Gerstner's] managerial talent more than they need his computer expertise," said one former CEO who knows him well.

Who's to blame for these revolutionary changes? A prominent New York lawyer who counsels many CEOs focused on the IBM board. "I think the directors are most subject to criticism," he said. "They've done nothing. IBM was the premier company in America. No company has had as much of a competitive edge. Nobody else was capable of competing with their state-of-the-art technology. But the company has just gone downhill and downhill. If I were to pick a negative example of the role of directors within a company, I would pick IBM because it is prototypical. With so many CEOs serving on its board, it's a club."

Yet the turmoil resulted from more than a failure of corporate governance. It grew from an inability to adjust to the latest phase in a whirlwind computer revolution, which IBM started. If ever a company and its board were stuck in the glory of their own history and their own familial culture, IBM was the case study. "GM and IBM are both number-one companies whose inward-looking cultures kept them from waking up in time," said GE consultant Noel Tichy.

The last seven days of January 1993 were as apocalyptic for CEOs as any week in American history. A corporate hat trick: Monday, out went Robinson. Tuesday, Akers. On Wednesday, Paul E. Lego of Westinghouse, once another standout in the industrial hall of fame.

Westinghouse Electric, the $14 billion-a-year company whose work ranges from defense contracts and energy systems, power engineering, broadcasting, and financial services, had been sliding into deep trouble. Its cash reserves and credit were depleted, its losses mounting, and its strategy fragmented. Lego, the lone-wolf CEO and chairman for less than three years, pleaded for time to straighten out the mess his predecessors had left. For months the sympathetic, clubby board went along.

Shareholders did not. Lego, 63, toured the country trying to reassure them. Calpers' general counsel, Richard H. Koppes, who describes himself as the "bad cop" in the "good-cop/bad-cop"

1991

Despite board allies, neither AmEx chairman and CEO James Robin-
son (left) nor Westinghouse chairman and CEO Paul Lego could fend
off shareholder complaints. Both men resigned in January 1993.

◆

team-up with his boss, Dale Hanson, said after a visit that "Lego
seemed to wallow in minutiae. He said the company's a mess and
it's not his fault." When Lego claimed he had a strong board,
noting such untamed, independent eminences as former defense
secretary Frank C. Carlucci, Koppes responded, "Yes, but he's
on many boards"; his capacity to concentrate on Westinghouse's
troubles was doubtful. (Carlucci is a recordholder: he sits on 20
company and 12 nonprofit boards. Second place: Vernon Jordan,
11 corporate boards, seven nonprofits.) According to a *Business
Week* reporter, Lego was "nearly in tears" at a meeting in Washington, D.C., with Richard V. Whitworth, president of United
Shareholders.

A *Business Week* editorial titled "Westinghouse's Do-Little
Board" complained that the directors were "yet another example of failed corporate governance," adding that "even though
the company was teetering on the brink of financial disaster, it
was investor pressure—not the board—that moved [Lego]."

There was no denying that the investors did move him. Ira
Millstein, the board's outside counsel, mediated, sitting in on
meetings with shareholders. One observer described how Mill-

stein worked: "He played a major role in advising the board, basically wiping out every anti-takeover device in the company. He said, Why do you have this stuff? If you want to keep in the good graces of the institutional shareholders, why not go the extra mile and make these changes?"

The board increased its meetings from five to 11 a year. And Lego agreed to radical changes in the board's composition, a reorganization of the company, and a new strategy of consolidation. Lego only "bought some time," warned Whitworth. Among the owners' unmet demands: that the board add more active directors and an independent chairman to oversee Lego.

Within weeks following his compromises, investor pressure forced Lego to quit. As the shareholders and Millstein had urged, an outside director, retired Amoco CEO Richard M. Morrow, was elected chairman of Westinghouse's board, while a group of other outside directors sought a replacement for Lego.

CEOs and their companies had become endangered species.

It was tempting to lay the blame on individuals (Stempel, Robinson, Akers, Lego). But their companies' slides were more attributable to cycles of change in business history, where new generations of enterprise (Microsoft, Wal-Mart, the Limited, McDonald's, Intel, Home Depot) succeeded the old.

Yet the decline signaled an accelerated evolution bordering on a revolution in the way the CEOs of troubled U.S. companies can expect to be treated in the future. "I think business is as mean as politics," joked Texas's spirited governor, Ann Richards, to a group of executives, "but you don't have to do it on the front page." Recent business history proved the first part of her wisecrack. But many an executive or board member in a laggard company could testify how wrong she was about the second part.

CEOs and directors could not miss the chilling headlines on page one and the covers of *The New York Times*, *The Wall Street Journal*, *The Washington Post*, the *Los Angeles Times*, *Business Week*, *Fortune*, or *Forbes*: ANATOMY OF A COUP: HOW ROBINSON LOST HIS JOB AS CEO…WAKE-UP CALL FOR CORPORATE BOARDS: WHAT'S GOOD FOR GENERAL MOTORS IS GOOD FOR THE COUNTRY…IBM CONCEDES ITS FAILURE TO ADAPT…DIRECTORS WAKE UP! INVESTORS ARE MAD AS HELL AND NOT GOING TO TAKE IT ANYMORE…SEARS ANNOUNCES SHIFTS ON GOVERNANCE POLICIES…MORE

POWER TO STOCKHOLDERS…TENSE TIMES: MORE CHIEF EXECU-
TIVES ARE BEING FORCED OUT BY TOUGHER BOARDS…BIG EXEC-
UTIVE SALARIES MAY MASK A BIGGER PROBLEM.

With press bloodhounds tracking every move, corporations, CEOs, and directors were as wary of media exposure as they were of lackluster stock performance or government intervention. Most would rather explain their actions to the SEC, IRS, or the Justice Department than be taken to task on the front pages of national or even local newspapers. At least government agencies had rules and formal avenues for reply. Take it from Michael Milken, who told a biographer in a jailhouse interview: "All these years I thought the marketplace or the customer was the final judge. I was wrong. In the short run, it's the media."

The First Amendment protects the press from the government. Increasingly, business editors and reporters with mixed motives invoke a new imperative: protecting the public from the secrecy surrounding what they judge to be the mistakes or duplicity of business. As much as the press hyped the stars of the moment, it reveled in making them fallen stars. Frank F. Mankiewicz, a Washington public-relations executive and former press secretary to Robert F. Kennedy, shares the view of many business reporters: "Politicians many be kiting checks or sleeping with contributors' wives, but they don't lie nearly as much as businessmen."

Not so long ago, CEOs of public companies could try to straighten troubles out in relative privacy. But increasingly, when shareholders found CEOs and companies unresponsive, they took their beefs to the press. In 1991, more than 25 companies tagged as "underperforming" by activist shareholders were on published lists for everyone to see. "We were like the Bad Housekeeping Seal of Disapproval," said Hanson of the increased publicity stirred by Calpers and other large investors. Ned Regan, New York's longtime comptroller, found that "the only way to be effective is to withhold your votes through the press."

The official newsletter of the National Association of Corporate Directors heralded the new era to its members: "Corporate governance in America is undergoing a true revolution of ideas. This intellectual revolution now occurring may be the most lasting legacy of these turbulent corporate times."

What caused the change? Are the forces behind it here to stay or just a passing nuisance to freewheeling corporate management?

THERE ARE PLENTY OF REASONS TO OWN A CITATION.
THIS ISN'T EVEN IN THE TOP TEN.

In a 1992 survey of top U.S. companies, the sales per employee for those operating aircraft were 26% greater than for those who did not. The net income was 102% greater. Financially rewarding reasons for flying one's own aircraft abound. And they are far more significant than escaping commercial airline inconvenience. There are even more reasons to make that aircraft a Citation. That's why, at 2,000 and growing, Citations form the largest fleet of business jets in the world.

THE SENSIBLE CITATIONS

Cessna
A Textron Company

Chapter Two

THE GOVERNING TRIANGLE: THEORY AND REALITY

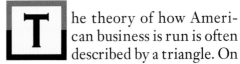

T he theory of how American business is run is often described by a triangle. On one side are the CEO and managers; on another, the board of directors; on the third, the shareholder-owners. The three sides intersect, symbolizing accountability in the business of public corporations.

In theory the CEO and his management run the company, responsible to the board of directors, which is accountable to the shareholder-owners. Hence the triangle—as tidy as an Aristotelian syllogism (major premise, minor premise, conclusion) or Hegel's triad for change (thesis, antithesis, synthesis). Each side of the triangle is dependent on the others for support. The shareholders elect the board. The board supervises the CEO and management. The CEO, within those limits, runs the company. A perfect system of checks and balances?

Hardly.

Like many tidy theories, this one has rarely worked in practice. What actually happens beggars the theory. The CEO most often picks the board that supervises him. The owners have been so fragmented that they had no feasible way to pressure, much less replace, their board representatives. Ninety-nine percent of directors slated by management are reelected each year—as easily as the minutes of the last meeting are approved. The option of shareholders' rejecting or electing their own directors "exists in theory," corporate counselor Martin Lipton affirmed, "but as a practical matter, it is not an effective way of dealing with corporate governance."

Even more conclusively, a policy paper from the United Shareholders pointed out, "The election of directors and resolution of issues are perfunctory exercises dominated and controlled by corporate managers. The theory of the publicly held corporation is not obsolete but, in practice, the corporate governance mechanism is."

Witness annual meetings of shareholders, the yearly display of corporate democracy at work. They are a theater of the absurd: the horseplay of token shareholders dressed in Batman costumes or football shoulder pads; shareholder filibusterers who make some senators of old seem like statesmen; a barrage of speeches disguised as questions from the perennial suspects; carefully rehearsed answers from managers; perfunctory block voting.

The meetings, where shareholders vote in elections or by proxy, have been campy farces. Discussions from the floor are often dominated by the likes of Evelyn Y. Davis, the attention-hungry flake who in April 1992 proclaimed to the struggling, very proper chairman of Citibank, John S. Reed, "I've got you by the balls." *The New York Times* reported that at the 1992 AmEx annual meeting "one shareholder approached the microphone wearing a clown's nose. Another kissed the chairman. Twice. It seemed almost an afterthought that the company's problems had any time on the agenda at yesterday's annual meeting."

Stockholder meetings "are the only forum that makes Congress look good by comparison," said shareholder activist Robert Monks. Corporate governance, complained a weary financial journalist, lies somewhere between rule by a military junta and rule by election in the old Supreme Soviet. Even so, as imperfect as it is, the American corporate system created the strongest and most democratic economy in the world. "Ours is more like a parliamentary system," said New York corporate lawyer Arthur Liman. "You don't get to vote for the prime minister. You vote for the party. Parliament is the board. But its membership is drawn from a list made up by the party."

Defenders of the system summon the trenchant aphorism about democracy, "Not a very good system, just the best there is." Shareholders, they say, also act as a disciplinary threat to fat and bad managers, who can be thrown out by embarrassed directors or rung out by predators waiting in the wings.

The erratic collective opinion of shareholders who measure by financial performance is preferable, the argument goes, to turning over control to the dictatorial wiles of managers. Said Richard F. Vancil, Harvard business professor and author of *Passing the Baton*, a casebook history of corporate succession: "A corporation is not a democracy that chooses its leader by popular vote. It has many constituencies that must be served."

The history of how American companies have been run is familiar. Entrepreneurial owners such as Henry Ford, Andrew Carnegie, and John D. Rockefeller and bankers such as J. P. Morgan and Andrew Mellon had few if any outside shareholders or ran their enterprises as if they thought they didn't. Government intervened only when their companies ran amok.

During and after World War II, American business was the envy of the world. Great Britain had lost its empire, and Germany and Japan, once the industrial heavyweights of Europe and Asia, were in ashes. American companies were spared the ravages of war. In the postwar era and beyond, they redirected their spectacular wartime production toward consumers in an eager worldwide market. Companies across the land were raking in record-breaking profits. For executives success was reflected in escalating pay packages and other rewards. Happy shareholders kept mum, watching the value of their stake multiply. "Back when there was no foreign competition," said GE's Jack Welch, "people were satisfied just to hang around."

To CEOs on both sides of the Atlantic, the theoretical power of boards of directors was a gentleman's joke. The proprietary publisher Henry R. Luce reflected on who was in charge of companies in the American economy: "It could not be any of the obvious constituencies. Not shareholders who cared only for profit. Not the board of directors, a small group of well-meaning but not necessarily wise gentlemen." No doubt about it. Like many other founders or families, the boss and his managerial heirs were unquestionably in charge.

ring to business as usual, a lord of the realm turesquely: "No effort of any kind is called irector]. You go to a meeting in a car sup-. You look both grave and sage and on two ee' and say 'I don't think so' once, and if £440. If you have five [directorships], it's having a permanent hot bath."

preneurs and managerial capitalists built they did a damn good job," says Ira Mill- nderful companies. Then something hap- pened. They were in power too long. They were unaccountable for too long. Their power became too great. The conglomerate movement [of the '60s] made them want to be even bigger. Our boards and everyone else forgot what they were supposed to be doing."

By the 1970s small fingers of doubt began to reach into the rosy sky. Global competition from countries the U.S. helped re- build were bedeviling some of America's leading industries. In most corporations professional managers, not proprietors, were in charge. Shareholder-owners remained mostly voiceless. Their board representatives were locked into the old buddy system.

Then the rambunctious '80s hit. Suddenly madness reigned in the corporate and financial world. The wildest decade of the modern business era jolted CEOs, boards, and shareholders into making decisions. Takeovers, mergers, leveraged buyouts, and junk bonds created a chaotic prosperity. Businesses and owners were making more money from money than from good, competitive products on the world market.

In all but the most egregious cases of self-serving deals, the courts took notice by enhancing the "business judgment rule." A cluster of decisions handed down by judges and chancellors affirmed that boards and management could override their share- holders' desire for quick short-term profits if they could prove thoughtful long-term objectives.

Thirty-nine state legislatures lobbied by business enacted statutes that made it harder to upend managers. When the courts and legislatures gave management and boards more leeway to perpetuate themselves, institutional investors began to rally. They wanted to share in the booty of the '80s. Their early ac- tivism formed over such issues as poison pills, shark repellents, and other gimmicks passed by boards to protect management and directors from raiders who offered shareholders bags of money.

Then almost overnight, in the last months of 1989, the deal decade collapsed into a pile of devalued paper. After 92 months of the largest business expansion in peacetime history and record employment, the debt engine imploded. Bankruptcies, criminal scandals, and corporate meltdowns littered the industrial and financial landscape. Who was to blame?

"In the 1990s politics will replace takeovers as the defining tool for [corporations], and a marketplace of ideas will replace the frenzied activity that dominated the financial marketplace in the 1980s," wrote Harvard professor John Pound. "Debate will replace debt as active shareholders identify specific operating policies for their target corporations and then invent new mechanisms to get their message across to management. To some observers the legacy of the 1980s is mainly a financial one. But seen in a broader context, the real legacy is *political*. Everyone involved now stands discredited to some degree: Wall Street for its greed; managers for their sloth; raiders for [their] predatory search for assets and callous disregard for the social costs."

Political?

Corporate politics evokes scenes of intrigue in executive suites, maneuvering for jobs and favor, or, on a lower level, whispered conferences at the water cooler and scenarios plotted over sandwiches in the company cafeteria. Not this time. The new politics of business sought a readjustment of the power structure—an effort to make the triangle of CEO, board, and shareholder more nearly equilateral. The movement challenged how some of America's biggest companies governed themselves. Shareholders asked directors to be more responsive to their concerns, to become more independent of and tougher on management. And they asked CEOs to understand that as chief executives they were managers, not owners or enthroned rulers.

The efforts to reshape the triangle, concluded Pound, "offer a sustainable middle ground between no governance and [too much] governance. The new politicized process is a system that Americans will support because it is in tune, perhaps for the first time, with the dictates of the American governance ideal."

When the system falters as it did in the '80s, business and its disciples learn lessons. The most obvious is that debt, leverage, and hostile takeovers produce more paper than products. Staying on that road could more easily lead to hell than Valhalla. A second lesson is that some of America's most radiant companies need to learn to compete again in world markets.

Another lesson of lasting value is less obvious: the methods for controlling and monitoring the affairs of corporations and their CEOs are undergoing momentous changes. CEOs need to adjust to the new climate or run nightmarish risks never dreamt of in their philosophy. "The trendy story in 1993 will be big shareholders, who have smelled blood at GM, Sears, and American Express, beating up on corporate management to be more responsive," wrote syndicated financial columnist Allan Sloan.

Who are these shareholders seizing power—a new species or just a mutation?

TO ONE CITATION OWNER, THIS LOOKS LIKE PERFECT FLYING WEATHER.

When one University of North Dakota pilot sees a thunderhead like this, he flies directly into it. It's part of his job as a weather researcher. So far, his specially equipped Citation has carried him, his copilot, and a scientist right into the jaws of 600 severe thunderstorms. And right back out again.

It's good to know that Citations can survive rough weather, but it's better to know they don't have to. Citations are built to cruise at altitudes far above most storm clouds. And most weather researchers.

THE SENSIBLE CITATIONS

Cessna
A Textron Company

Chapter Three

ENTER THE SHAREHOLDERS

T he 50 million shareholders of American public companies were once as placid and aimless as plankton in a rising sea. From the earliest stirrings of the capitalist enterprise system, shareholder-owners nourished business with their money. But they rarely swam together unless predators forced them to. For the first time, in the late 1980s and '90s they began to form into groups and turn on their hosts. In their new formation, they started putting their mouths where their money was.

As individuals, the multitude of new shareholders each held small stakes. They were patronized for years as myrmidon "widows and orphans." They could have a voice in how companies were run only by banding together. But they lacked the ties that bind. In their often quoted 1932 classic *The Modern Corporation and Private Property*, two Columbia University professors, lawyer Adolf A. Berle Jr. and economist Gardiner C. Means, legitimized the split between professional managers and the hundreds of thousands of new owners. By buying tokens called shares, the authors said, the owners ceded their voting rights to the managers. If the management failed to please them, the owners could sell their shares and buy into another company.

Putative owners in name only had climbed aboard accelerating company bandwagons, along for the enriching ride. Nobody expected them to get near the wheel. After all, what could they know about driving a company, other than to revel in its tracks of green?

Advancing technology, government regulation, and new financial techniques made investing a more complex specialty. For decisions, small individual investors turned increasingly to investment and pension funds. In 1976, Peter Drucker described the transformation in the title of his book *The Unseen Revolution: How Pension Fund Socialism Came to America*. Not socialism—the change was more accurately a gestating new democracy in the American economic system. But it lacked democracy's defining seed: the people's voice.

Shareholders were a mute mass. In their 1992 *Director's Monthly* article, Washington lawyers Ralph C. Ferrara and Harry Zirlin describe the "demographic shift away from numerous isolated and small shareholders to a relatively few unified large shareholders. Prior to the merger market in the 1980s, with its allure of large premiums over market price of 'target' corporations, institutional investors abided by the 'Wall Street Rule.'" They sold their stock, the authors continued, reasoning that influencing the corporation would cost more than "voting with their feet."

The shift in ownership concentration and objectives quickened more like a tidal wave than a groundswell. In 1950, funds owned not much more than 8 percent of American companies. By 1993, institutional funds owned close to 60 percent of the shares in enterprises of the whole American industrial and service economy. "What finished off corporate capitalism [when management was in complete control] was the emergence of the 'institutional investor,'" wrote Drucker in 1992. For the first time, analysts began referring to "real owners" instead of just "owners."

Most transformations in the power structure of business creep up over decades. What suddenly made shareholders think of themselves not just as investors but as "real owners"?

Anyone could see that shares once held by individuals had moved to their surrogates, pension and investment funds. No decennial census was needed to spot the trend. Statistics and graphs poured out every month highlighting the change. Initially the new concentration of money didn't make much difference. The biggest funds were like nation-states. They had common interests but no common voice. Their behavior more closely reflected their old impotence than their latent new power.

SEC rules prevented shareholders from collaborating for their common benefit without hobbling registration and dense disclosure requirements. The government considered shareholders potentially too powerful to allow the funds easy joint action. Government had released business from the most stringent antitrust laws. Yet it continued to prevent the institutional investors, presumably the partners of corporate America, from exercising their collective strength. Said Richard C. Breeden, SEC chairman for the last two years of the Bush administration, "Shareholders have been muzzled by federal law."

In the past they had expressed themselves financially. They chucked losers and embraced more appealing partners. But the richer the funds became—the larger their attachments to thousands of companies—the more expensive it became for them to be such fickle suitors.

Commissions and other transaction fees were costly. Most big funds lacked the staff or resources to make selective investment calls. Thousands of proxies flowed into their offices every month unmined and in many cases unopened. The price of the stock in any quarter or year had to be the bottom line, no matter how bad a measure of real value it might be over a longer period. Valuation without representation was the stockholders' fate.

But the bingeing of the junky '80s laid low both the high-flying adventurers and the investors who followed them. They suffered a paralyzing hangover. Where could they turn? Proxy fights, shareholder resolutions, and lawsuits were expensive and bootless ways to express dissatisfaction with poor company performance.

Fecklessly, funds and some individual activists continued filing protests in proxies over such social issues as the environment, divestment of companies that did business in South Africa, equal opportunity. More significant, they had also begun to register complaints against what they regarded as management's dictatorship over the affairs of corporate America. They clamored for shareholders' rights: more responsive directors and a say in preventing management locks such as nonvoting stock or the staggered election of boards.

They hungered to use their voices to influence rather than their feet to walk away. In the fashionable buzzword of other protest movements, they vainly sought more "empowerment" than the stacked ballot boxes of theoretical corporate democracy. As in most entrenched dictatorships, at first the "people" routinely lost, savoring a pitiful gain in supporting votes. Annual meetings were even more useless forums scripted by the management, whose biggest allies were long-winded regulars, the monopolizers of the corporate town meetings.

One flash point ignited the firestorm of shareholder activism. The incendiary issue was executive pay.

As with so many epochal reformations, this change began with a symbolic spark rather than a bonfire. The public became outraged at management's high living. In a series of headline-making disclosures, what the press and shareholders alike called "executive greed" was personified in print and on TV with names and dollar signs. Shareholders of many companies saw that no matter how companies were doing, top executive salaries, stock options, and bonuses had reached heights that would have embarrassed Croesus. "Pay for performance," not for goofing became the security owners' cry. "A Game of Greed," shouted a 1988 *Time* cover story.

The widespread indignation erupted first over the planned $100 million reward to RJR Nabisco's roguish CEO, F. Ross Johnson, in his attempted management buyout of the company. (Instead he was kicked out, pocketed a mere $53.8 million, and still sits on the AmEx and four other boards.) That revelation was followed by calculations that Warner Communications' CEO, Steven J. Ross, already nicknamed the Babe Ruth of executive pay, was collecting compensation of $79 million in one year as part of the $200 million package he received for merging his company with Time Inc. (with the potential of hundreds of millions more in new options). To many the pay packages seemed to reflect, in the words of the leading compensation expert Graef S. Crystal, a "Marie Antoinette School of Management."

Louis Lowenstein, author of *Sense and Nonsense in Corporate Finance* and director of Columbia University's Institutional Investor Project, underscores the allusion to "Let them eat cake": "The monarchs of *ancien régime* Europe claimed God was their source of power. Modern-day CEOs are only slightly more humble. They recognize that, under law, the shareholders are supreme, but they then nullify that supremacy, saying investors lack the competence to give advice about the business. Power without accountability to someone in particular is not accountable at all, and our entire economic system is organized in a way that makes shareholder interests primary."

The royal isolation of CEOs and their boards of courtiers, barricaded in corporate castles, had been under attack by their shareholder masses since the late '80s. The assault was still mostly mounted in lame proxy-statement pleadings and beefs to the press. They rarely had much effect. But by 1991, resolutions objecting to management and board practices were hurled at company parapets with new force. Yet after tallying the votes at the annual meetings, management still prevailed.

Dissenting votes slowly increased. In some rare instances the shareholders won or at least embarrassed the boards and managers into taking action. Even though indifferent proxies collected by management overwhelmed the protest votes, a vote of less than 90 percent for management was a sure sign of trouble. "I know of no board," said Bruce Atwater of the Business Roundtable, "that would not be moved dramatically if as little as 20 percent of the shareholders' vote was withheld for the election of directors."

The largest fund, Calpers of California, represents more than 900,000 beneficiaries. It decided on a different tactic, what it called a "kinder, gentler" approach. Calpers would try persuasion rather than confrontation. Other funds quickly joined in.

"We weren't going around trying to rape corporate America," said Dale Hanson of Calpers. "In the past we had sort of been like little gnats. Companies just brushed us away. But if they happened to be poor performers, all of a sudden they were facing a swarm of angry bees." Not that many of the shareholder groups approached CEOs and boards of directors with threats. "When we said we wanted to talk," Hanson pointed out, "we didn't file a resolution at the same time. We really wanted to talk. The good news was that we were no longer filing flaky resolutions on saving the whales or chickens. We were focusing on poorly per-

1988

In 1991, when 10 out of 12 companies refused to meet with Calpers, its chief executive, Dale Hanson, took his concerns to the press. The following year, Calpers' new "dirty dozen" all agreed to meet.

◆

forming companies. It is our stated objective to ensure an equal-sided triangle. We want directors to represent interests of all the shareholders. Unless we can see some economic tie back to them, we are not going to pursue an issue."

A phone call or letter to a CEO from any of the big funds requesting a meeting was once about as welcome as hearing from Mike Wallace that *60 Minutes* wanted to do a piece on the company.

Many CEOs were put off, saying to themselves and to their directors, "What do these guys know about our business?" When Calpers asked for an audience with the CEO W. J. Sanders III of Advanced Micro Devices, an electronics company with revenues of $1.5 billion in which the fund owned a large stake, "we got back a three- or four-page letter," recalled Hanson, "that basically said, 'Up yours. I don't need you. Meet with my investor relations guy.'" The initial reaction of many CEOs was to protect themselves from critics. Hanson recalls getting the cold shoulder from Edwin I. Colodny, former CEO of US Air, then hemmed in by takeover threats. They met in 1989 in a hangar at Washington National Airport. "At first he was hostile and defensive," said Hanson. He recalled Colodny asking, "Okay, who do you want us to be taken over by?" Hanson explained that was not Calpers' game. "Colodny lightened up. He realized that we didn't want to throw the company to the wolves." Calpers' intention was simply to hear how Colodny planned to save US Air. When he and Hanson parted 90 minutes later, Colodny passed out US Air key chains to the Calpers group.

Even a simple gesture like writing a board about concerns could raise a CEO's ire. Hanson recalled writing the GM board following Roger Smith's 1989 retirement announcement. "We said, You are about to undertake the single most important function you will ever undertake: the hiring of a CEO. How are you going to evaluate this person over the next three-, five-, or 10-year period? How are you going to maintain your relationship with your shareholders?"

Smith objected, saying Calpers was interfering with the hiring process. "He basically told us to go to hell without checking with the board," said Hanson. "At the next meeting, the directors told Roger he had to meet with us—these are important people."

In 1991 Calpers targeted 12 companies whose problems it wanted to discuss. Quietly, its officers asked for meetings with American Express, Chrysler, Control Data, Dial, Ryder, Hercules, IBM, ITT, Polaroid, Salomon Brothers, Time Warner, and US Air. "But when we took the kinder, gentler approach, most basically thumbed their noses at us," said Koppes of Calpers. Ten of the 12 did not respond.

Rejection did not last long. Another powerful way to get the companies' attention was at hand. The 12 quickly found themselves spotlighted as arrogant by *Business Week*, *Fortune*, *The New York Times*, and *The Wall Street Journal*. "That [coverage] certainly got everybody motivated to get together," said Daniel R. Pennie, then general counsel for Control Data. Before long, every company on the list agreed to talk. Similarly, United Shareholders was negotiating with other companies on its list over questions of governance, duplicating many of Calpers' targets.

A year later, in 1992, when Calpers went to its new dirty dozen, the response was different. All the companies that had not already responded favorably immediately agreed to meet, offering not only their CEOs but their directors as well. By 1993 even "Up Yours" Sanders agreed to several of Calpers' key governance proposals.

"My perspective on Calpers," said Bruce Atwater, "is that it is a positive force. It started out on social issues like South Africa. It migrated to issues like staggered boards. And now it is on to the real issue, which is performance." Added Hanson, "When CEOs and board members finally did sit down with us, they discovered we didn't have horns and a tail."

The fund managers and shareholder groups insisted they were not trying to tell CEOs or directors how they should run their companies. "We're not micromanagers," said former New York state comptroller Ned Regan. "I firmly believe we ought not to be involved in management. We have to start out trusting companies and then hold the boards accountable to have a check on that trust." Ralph Whitworth of United Shareholders agreed. "We would make a wreck out of corporate America if we tried to run it by plebiscite," he said. At their best the shareholder groups seemed not to be telling sinking companies what to do. They conceded that in most cases they didn't know. Their message was: Do something or get out of the way.

Robert A. G. Monks, founder of Institutional Shareholders Services, who successfully fought for a reorganization of Sears and its board, summed up the objective of many shareholder activists: "Hey, there are owners. We can read and write. We can distinguish between issues that are in our long-term interest and those that are against our long-term interest. We want to call to your attention that we have come back, that there is such a thing as an owner. And we want to talk with you about how we can best work together to make the capitalist system work the way it was intended."

Are institutional investors really that high-minded? Many readily admit they are not. Certainly CEOs and directors agree that shareholders often send out mixed signals.

IN REAL LIFE, THE HARE BEATS THE TORTOISE EVERY TIME.

For years, the turboprop industry has claimed that slow and steady wins the race. To say that a turboprop is somehow more sensible than a jet is a harebrained notion at best. At nearly 100 mph faster, the Citation II outperforms turboprops in every category, at operating costs guaranteed to be lower. And for virtually the same purchase price.

Today, the turboprop story is little more than a fairy tale. And the time has come, once and for all, to close the book on it.

THE SENSIBLE CITATIONS

Cessna
A Textron Company

Chapter Four

TRADERS VERSUS INVESTORS

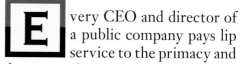very CEO and director of a public company pays lip service to the primacy and welfare of shareholders and even to their role in corporate affairs. The doctrine of the governance triangle demands it. But in truth most managements regard active shareholders as an intrusive damn nuisance, despite obligatory maxims to the contrary.

Senior executives in America repeatedly affirm that their highest goal is "maximizing *shareholder* value." What they most often mean is, Let *us* decide how to achieve that goal, and shareholders will be better off.

Louis Lowenstein of Columbia University nailed the myth. In a 1991 letter to a friend, reported Lowenstein, Thomas A. Murphy, CEO of GM in its halcyon days, vented his spleen at holy shareholder-owners: "Many so-called investors [are] nothing more than predators, opportunists, speculators, traders, arbitragers, scavengers, even blackmailers, whose focus is on nothing more than trying to capitalize on the short-term profit to them regardless of the consequences."

An old-fashioned crotchety view? Of course. But deep down it is not so far from the feeling of many a modern CEO.

Too simple, said corporate lawyer Martin Lipton. "The real debate is not about maximizing value; it's about the time frame. The people who run these companies are generally good managers. They're not bad people. They're honest. What you have is a tug-of-war between a shareholder group that has grown larger and larger, exerting extreme pressure to get short-term performance, and managers who feel they best maximize shareholder value by having enterprises that grow steadily over a period of time."

The core problem is traders versus investors.

Replacing the giant proprietary tycoons or their families is a shareholder larger than any in American history: the institutional fund, a juggernaut representing in one portfolio hundreds, thousands, or even a million shareholders.

No single person or family has ever been as rich in shares or capital as any one of the biggest investment funds. Analysts consider that a shareholder who can vote 15 percent or more in any company has working control. "If 30 of these fund managers ever decided to sit down in a room together, they could probably control corporate America," says lawyer Ira Millstein. "You have to say to yourself, *What does that mean?* That concentration of ownership is very important. We're basically a country that has never liked concentration."

At the largest public companies, institutional holdings account for close to 60 percent of the stock. And in companies whose stock they consider prime—GM, AT&T, Capital Cities/ABC, and Amoco, among others—funds own up to 80 or 90 percent of total shares. To be sure, except in some smaller companies, a single fund rarely owns as much as 2 percent of a company. But if they got together?

Now they have.

In October 1992, new SEC regulations suddenly transformed little David shareholders into unshackled Goliaths. The SEC freed most shareholders with a common purpose to join forces without jumping through regulatory hoops. It also enabled them to cherry pick individual directors of their choice rather than vote for or against the entire slate proposed by management. Finally, it dealt with executive pay not by limits but by requiring clearer disclosure.

Former SEC chairman Richard Breeden described the ukase as "a watershed for corporate governance intended to empower shareholders." As part of the new rules freeing up shareholders, the SEC also required clear language and understandable charts that reflected the pay and benefits of key executives. Obfuscation had become such a widespread corporate practice that few CEOs could complain about the new "sunshine" illuminating executive compensation.

Corporate managers were far less tranquil about the effect of freeing the big shareholders to act in concert. They had good reason to be wary.

Shareholder funds were no more white-hatted than the black-hatted managers and boards they often railed against. "Bringing more democracy to corporate governance" had a nice theoretical ring to it. But in practice it was as blemished as the board and managerial domination it opposed.

1988

New SEC regulations, pushed through in October 1992 by former chairman Richard Breeden, freed shareholders to join forces.

Money managers, who invest on behalf of individuals in pension or mutual funds and trusts, insist their role in the system is to force managements and boards to give them—the owners—the biggest possible return on their investment. Indeed, they argue, it's more than a right. In many instances they have a legal *duty* to get the most for their investors' money. The law calls it their fiduciary duty.

Some describe it as speculator capitalism. Said Michael E. Porter, professor of business administration at Harvard Business School: "Because of laws and regulations that prod funds to be prudent and spread their investment risks, the big institutions each typically hold small stakes of a percent or so in hundreds and even thousands of different companies. And they trade with increasing frequency." The average holding period of stocks has declined from more than seven years in 1960 to two years in 1993.

A few large private funds turn over their portfolios 100 percent or more every year. Many investment managers make their money on commissions rather than long-term measurements of their success or failure. "Bear in mind that there's a whole business that depends on people switching their investments from one company to another," said Lipton. "Unless you have this turnover, you don't have a brokerage business."

"I'm deeply concerned," said Treasury secretary Lloyd Bentsen, "about the churning of stocks and short-term horizons." Investment banker Felix G. Rohatyn shared the concern: "Speculative behavior is not driven by individuals as it was in the 1920s but by such institutions as pension funds, banks, savings and loans, and insurance companies."

Critics argue that the short-term grab for profit has hurt American competitiveness in the world market. But the biggest public pension funds plead not guilty to taking their money and running. They are long-term investors, most insist. They have to be. Many are 80 to 100 percent "indexed."

Funds are indexed when they make the same weighted selections of stocks as the overall market measures—Standard & Poor's 500, the Dow Jones, or the Wilshire 5000 or the Russell 2000 indexes. More than 80 percent of public pension-fund investments are thus automatic. They tend not to be short-termers, buying and holding for at least seven to 10 years. Companies like IBM, GM, AT&T, Exxon, and many Fortune 500 companies are in everybody's index.

Since over long periods the market has always risen, indexing is the least chancy way of investing. Only a Cassandra predicting a permanent decline in the world economy could disagree. "It's an expression of market efficiency," said a financial journalist. "No one can predict with any certainty which way the market will go, so why not just go with it." Indexed shareholders have been dubbed "stuckholders." One stand-pat manager of a small mutual fund shares their conservative view. "To buy a new stock," he said, "I have to sell one. That means I can make two mistakes."

Indexing has other important appeals for pension funds. Since they hold rather than actively trade shares, they pay relatively few brokerage commissions. For example, if a fund chose to replace its 1 percent stake in GM (worth more than $300 million), the transaction costs could be as much as $3 million. Unloading such large blocks could also depress the market. Nor do most of the funds have the staffs to examine the thousands of proxies they receive each year. One estimate is that management fees and transaction costs can eat as much as 20 percent of investors' market gains. So the index funds go with the market, historically up over the long run. Remember the careful gambler on the way to the racetrack who said, "Boy, I sure hope I break even today. I need the money." Index investing is similar to the limited expectations of that prudent bettor.

Call it prudence or inflexibility, the "stuck" position of index funds has more or less forced the funds to share a bed with management—unlike small investors, who can easily move in and out of the market. The harder it became for investors to exchange shares, the more likely the new management-shareholder tug-of-war became.

Index funds and other holders of large amounts of stock call themselves "passive" investors or, in the best circumstances, "relationship" investors. Relationship investors are those that actually track companies, holding their shares and becoming involved with management and boards rather than simply buying and selling the way "active" investors do. Relationship investors are long-term holders who try to spot early signs of trouble and attempt to collaborate with the board and CEO on long-term solutions.

Since the biggest public funds each own such a small share of so many companies, what right or reason do they have to try to influence any one of them?

Lee Iacocca, former CEO and chairman of Chrysler, wondered just that when he first met with Dale Hanson of Calpers. Iacocca snorted that Chrysler never paid any attention to Calpers because the fund would hold onto Chrysler's stock whether it rose or not. "He was quite annoyed," said Hanson. And why not? "Having sworn off short-termism, funds are now asking for more respect," Louis Lowenstein pointed out. "But how can funds locked into an index be treated with respect when they are driven by a formula?"

Ask CEOs why they bother to meet with shareholders who own only 1 or 2 percent of their companies, and they all give the same automatic answer: "We talk to *any* of our big shareholders." But institutional funds—Calpers, the Council of Institutional Investors, United Shareholders, Institutional Shareholders Services, or any big state and city pension fund—are not just any shareholders. Together the funds can represent a controlling interest in the company. Now that the relaxed SEC rules

THE CITIZENS OF ONLY ONE CONTINENT ON EARTH HAVE YET TO RELY ON THE CITATION V.

Across six continents and 38 countries, the Citation V is the fastest-selling business jet in history. It outsells all other competing aircraft – jet or turboprop – because it outperforms them in so many ways. Yet its operating costs are guaranteed to be lower than any competing airplane.

Year after year, on financial statements throughout the world, the Citation V is one bird that looks very good in black and white.

THE SENSIBLE CITATIONS

allow funds to act in concert, their power is even greater. Nell Minow, an influential shareholder-rights advocate who runs a small nonindexed investment fund with activist Robert Monks, says that when she talks to a director or CEO of a company, her attitude is, "We may have had a shotgun wedding, but we're still married." (Indexed pension funds, for instance, had a $1.85 billion paper loss from IBM's one-year decline alone.) Still, Minow notes a dramatic change in CEO attitudes toward investors. "In the past most CEOs ignored us or tried to pass us on to the second assistant to the deputy investor-relations guy," said Minow. "Now we get phone calls from the CEOs. The ones who have been through the shadow of the valley of death know that getting along with shareholders probably beats the alternative."

Hanson, who says he hates indexing, is trying to move more of Calpers' portfolio into more active management, reducing the number of companies it holds from 2,000 to 700 or 800. New York's Ned Regan explored better ways to evaluate companies by a "sampling approach." Even without such a switch, Calpers, the most prominent fund seeking to influence corporate behavior, carries a big stick. "If you happen to be a bad performer, you're not just on our list," said Hanson. "You're likely to be on the lists of 15 or 20 funds."

Once it took millions of dollars in mailings for a complaining shareholder to reach all the others who held shares. Now, by getting in touch with a handful of funds, the same can be accomplished at little or no cost. Said one business journalist, "A bandleader like Dale Hanson, whose salary is $95,000 a year, can be as powerful a player as J. P. Morgan, who played solo on his golden trumpet."

But public funds are not as free of shackles as they may seem. Many are run by elected or politically appointed officials. Calpers' board, for example, has 13 members: four are named by the governor, one by state legislators, and two others are the elected state treasurer and controller. The California state legislature requires that Calpers' investments be "South Africa-free" to protest apartheid. Other special-interest groups and politicos lean on public funds as well. No matter what their views, state and city funds must lobby legislatures, politicians, and activists who can force them to divest companies whose social and political policies come under attack.

It is merciful that the bigger public funds see their role as focusing on corporate procedures—governance of lethargic companies—rather than on operations. Few shareholders want to manage. They want their investments protected and enhanced. To ensure that, they ask for better representation through the boards, which serve as their surrogates. But even those who insist on such limited demands send mixed signals. Are their interests long term or short? Is their judgment based purely on financial returns, on computer analysis and indexes that offer little insight into the company players, their integrity, the quality of their strategies, or the likelihood of their success?

Who are the leaders of these new powerhouse funds? How and by what criteria do they make *their* decisions? Is their size and concentration as much a threat to competition in the share marketplace as monopolies and oligopolies are in business?

Managers and directors have long ruled American corporate life. Shareholders are now ineluctably extending and shoring up their own side of the governing triangle. But like managers and directors who have too often abused their authority or neglected their duty, shareholders as a group must move carefully in exerting their new influence. Together in their investment groups, which now dominate the economy, they have more than increased clout. They have a responsibility to use that new enfranchisement wisely.

Most funds realize that long-range plans like increasing capital for research and development won't immediately improve quarterly results. But Irving S. Shapiro, former chairman of Du Pont and the Business Roundtable, warns: "Institutional investors can be indifferent to any corporate interests except current stock values and dividends. They march to a different drummer. They need results this year or this quarter, or they lose their [individual] investors and their jobs. To put it bluntly, the system is driven by fees and short-term profits. We need new traffic signals to make the system work better."

Avarice is one engine in the enterprise system. But it is not the only one.

IF THERE WERE A CITATION FAMILY REUNION,
THE GROUP PHOTO WOULD LOOK LIKE THIS.

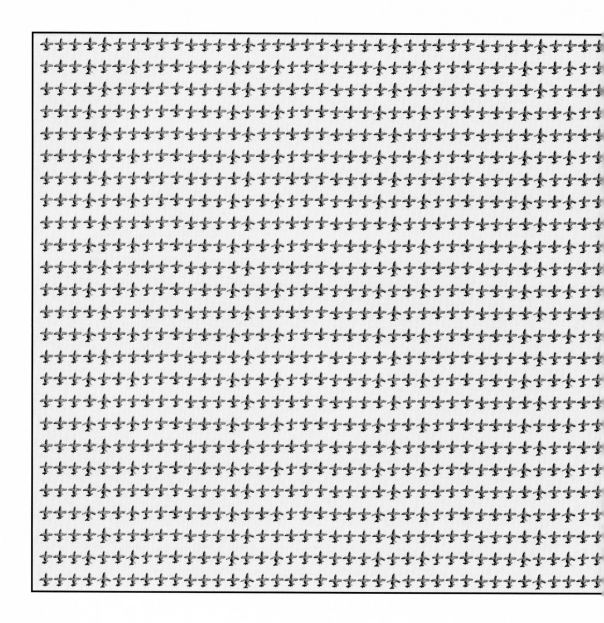

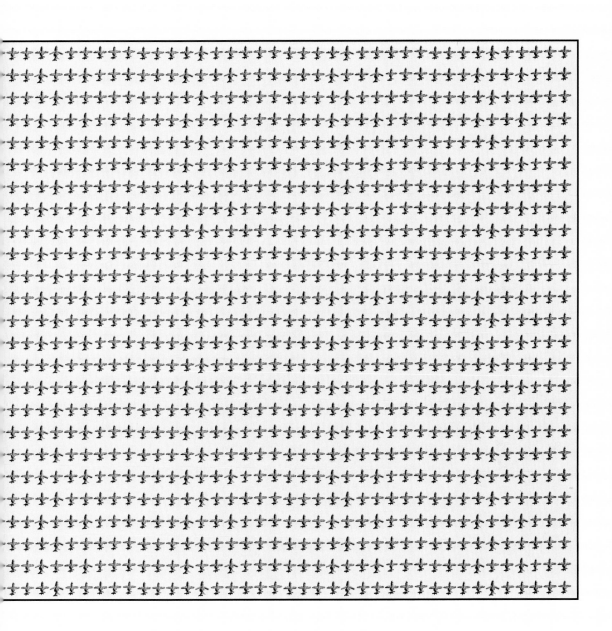

When the first Citation was delivered in 1972, its competitors had a
big head start. They'd been selling in the same market for nearly a decade.

But buyers know a superior product when they see one. And they
began buying Citations. Today, the worldwide Citation fleet has grown
to 2,000 and counting. The Citation family has expanded to six models.

And something else keeps growing larger and larger, too. Citation's
lead over those competitors who had that big head start.

THE SENSIBLE CITATIONS

Chapter Five

You're Still the Boss: Now What?

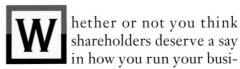hether or not you think shareholders deserve a say in how you run your business, they have one. So what do you do about it? How do you avoid the gilded plank your CEO peers are walking in increasing numbers?

The growth in the power of institutional investors has forced many CEOs into vigorous self-examination. How am I doing with *my* board and shareholders? Am I paying enough attention to their concerns? Am I a good listener or an autocratic SOB? Have I put too many golf chums on the board? Or do I have rigorous, independent directors who push me past self-congratulation? Do I weigh the shareholders' relatively short-term goals fairly against longer-term company interests?

George M. C. Fisher, chairman and CEO of Motorola, the fast-moving electronics manufacturer, puts issues of governance in perspective. "Those of us in industry need to look in a mirror very carefully," he said. "Ninety percent of the competitiveness issue has to do with execution within the corporation— paying attention to customers and to delivery of the highest quality product at the lowest cost. If every company concentrated on those fundamentals and could explain them to all its publics, much of our competitiveness issue would go away."

Fisher is emblematic of successful CEOs like Jack Welch of GE who get little quarrel from their admiring boards. "Their meetings are more like pep rallies than board meetings," said one observer of both companies.

Still, explaining fundamentals to constituencies like your board can be a sticky business. Admiral James F. Calvert, an active director and the chairman of Aqua-Chem, a Milwaukee-based manufacturer of boilers and treatment systems, describes four kinds of governance situations:

• Everything is bliss. The company is profitable, with an honest CEO who lets the board participate. Problems are solved in a businesslike way.

• Everything is almost bliss. The company is well run and profitable. The CEO wants nothing from the board except its ear and its support. Any attempt at independent thinking is quietly but firmly squashed.

• Everything is not great. The company is not profitable enough. The CEO wants advice from everybody but is not sure of anything when he gets it. The board tries but isn't able to help. The situation is frustrating but not dangerous—yet.

• Almost everything looks terrible. The company is losing money at a frightening rate. The CEO acts as if he owns the company but is unable to rectify matters.

No matter where he falls on the spectrum, a CEO can no longer just stick to his business. His newly assertive constituencies— board, shareholders, government, media, employees, customers— are his business. They all require attention if he is to survive. The old pol's maxim applies: You can be a peacock one day and a feather duster the next.

More than ever in American corporate history, powerful watchdogs circle the CEO. The press, which in the past decade has discovered that business news can be as juicy as politics or sports, reports every move a major CEO makes. "Thirty years ago the business press was far more docile," said public policy adviser David Sawyer. "Today business is covered by a diverse collection of aggressive reporters who understand that uncovering a corporate scandal is the shortest route to journalistic success."

Even successful, attentive CEOs have no guarantee of longevity. "You're not likely to test umbrellas when the sun is shining," said Louis Lowenstein of Columbia University. It might be a good idea. Not only shareholders but boards have become impatient with slow-moving, if self-assured, CEOs. Lee Iacocca, who brought Chrysler back from Armageddon, is a painful albeit familiar example of one who ignored this primary rule: do not assume success brings perpetual rule. In his desire to stay on top and his refusal to choose a successor, Iacocca asserted indispensability—much as William S. Paley of CBS or Armand Hammer of Occidental Petroleum once did. The result: Iacocca drained the board's goodwill. His directors replaced him with a candidate from GM, denying Iacocca the status he sought as a kind of Henry Ford II. "Imperial rule," commented *The New York Times*, "is fading fast."

Sunbeam-Oster CEO Paul B. Kazarian also neglected his flanks, depending too heavily on past laurels. Despite two years of rising company earnings and stock value, the four outside directors on his board, including former SEC chairman Roderick M. Hills, suddenly fired the CEO in January 1993. Protesting Kazarian's Queeg-like management, a group of key executives threatened to jump ship unless the board acted.

Nor did a radiant past help Compaq CEO Joseph "Rod" Canion, who lost out after watching his company rise close to the top in advanced-design desktop and portable computers. In 1991, when the company floundered, Benjamin M. Rosen, Compaq's chairman and Canion's close friend, led the ouster. Ekhard Pfeiffer, chief operating officer, replaced Canion and by 1993 raised profits 63 percent.

"The lack of sentimentality," said one prominent director of these board-led dismissals, "is spreading every day."

So how do present-day CEO wizards prevent a fall? The wisest recognize their powerful constituencies and invite them into their camp.

Henry B. Schacht, 58, a prominent director and business leader, is CEO of Cummins Engine, a Columbus, Indiana, company known for quality diesel engines and power systems as well as outstanding employee relations and community service. Schacht became CEO in 1973, during a period of rapid growth for the company. Cummins had record profits and earnings. But when he looked ahead to the '80s and '90s, he saw that Japanese competition could threaten the strengths that had driven company growth for 30 years.

Schacht's board and major shareholders agreed to invest $1 billion in research even though the company's stock market value was only $250 million. By the '80s, Japanese competition had, as predicted, forced Cummins to cut its prices in order to gain market share. As a result, profits declined, and in 1987 the company began to lose money.

Schacht again persuaded Cummins' major investors to support his long-range plan and to retain their stock for at least six years. He encouraged large investors to join the company's board and refused employment contracts for himself and other executives. Schacht met often with shareholders, their representatives, employees, and others who had a stake in the company "because I wanted them to feel like real owners." The company had operating profits again in 1992, and those continued to rise in 1993. Explained Schacht: "You've got to ask, 'What does it take to run a corporation? Who are the people who have a stake? Who has primacy, if anybody? Whose company is it anyway?'"

One CEO for whom the answer came hard is Edward A. Brennan of Sears. The third generation of Brennans to spend his working life at Sears, he resisted the first investor grumblings in 1990. But ducking complaints over Sears' avalanche of bad news proved impossible. Said Rawleigh Warner, former Mobil CEO and dissident AmEx director: "Sam Walton just ate Sears' lunch every time Sears turned around."

One of the first to offer suggestions from outside the company was Robert Monks, originator of Institutional Shareholder Services, whose staff reviews 5,400 proxy statements a year and recommends how shareholders should vote. In a meeting with Sears and a group of investors that included Calpers, Monks urged Brennan to reorganize the board so that it could help him remodel the company.

When Monks tried to join the Sears board himself, Brennan and the directors blocked him. "Monks was not the kind of director we needed," said Sears general counsel David Shute. "We really need our directors to focus primarily on financial performance. We regard governance issues as a distraction."

Brennan stubbornly resisted the new realities of corporate

governance. "The vote was in no way a defeat," he said, referring to mounting proxies that were recorded against the company's management and board at the May 1992 annual meeting. "I can't conceive why people should even think that way."

One month after the negative vote and a year after the rancor began, Sears and its board realized they couldn't beat the shareholders. Acceding to four demands, they agreed to:
- Enable all shareholders to vote confidentially.
- Require every director to own at least 1,000 shares of Sears stock.
- Change the directors' retirement age from 78 to 72.
- Compose the nominating committee of outside directors only.

Brennan had learned to sing his constituents' song. "The board," he admitted, "has listened to our shareholders."

Assailed by shareholder complaints and dwindling earnings, Sears agreed to spin off its financial service businesses and to concentrate on merchandising. As another peace offering, Brennan hired an executive recruiting firm to consult with institutional shareholders on board nominees.

Brennan kept a low profile while Arthur C. Martinez, the new merchandising chief brought in from Saks Fifth Avenue, reorganized the company. Sears' venerated 97-year-old catalog was abolished, and 113 unprofitable stores were closed and 50,000 jobs cut. "It's a nice start," said Monks. "It's helpful to have responsiveness any time." But United Shareholders wasn't satisfied. It has again urged shareholders to approve a proxy proposal preventing Brennan from serving as both CEO and chairman. A similar effort a year earlier led by the New York state pension fund had won approval from 27 percent of shareholders.

"The dreary Sears case is a hard-earned lesson reminiscent of Richard Nixon trying to tough it out," said one financial writer. "The CEO and board can no longer just dig in their heels when shareholders, press, and damning evidence of mismanagement demand change."

According to Brennan, Sears now "has a more forward-looking position." But any look backward shows that Brennan and many members of his board shunned early warning from their shareholders. They got stuck in the torpor of their old retailing habits, which toppled them from number one in the field while

PETER UEBERROTH SAW HIS NEW CITATION CABIN ON THIS SCREEN FOUR MONTHS BEFORE IT WAS ACTUALLY BUILT.

When entrepreneur Peter Ueberroth came to Cessna to select his new interior, we showed him hundreds of beautiful fabric and hardwood options. Moments later, we showed him something even better – a realistic simulation of his Citation cabin, with all his choices "installed."

This computer visualization system is just one of many surprising innovations at Cessna's new Customer Center. And it's one reason why our owners face no surprises at all when their Citations are completed.

THE SENSIBLE CITATIONS

Cessna
A Textron Company

discount chains and specialty stores thrived. With the purchase of Dean Witter and Coldwell Banker in 1981, Sears had also plunged into a massive and disastrous financial services diversification (mocked as a "socks and stocks" strategy), while their stores and catalog moldered. Sears director Donald H. Rumsfeld, a former secretary of defense, admitted the board was slow to act. "Some board members came to agreement well back and others more recently," he said. The new Sears "will have greater flexibility and a tightened business focus," Brennan wanly told his employees by videotape. "We are at last concentrating on our core business."

Not all CEOs have had such painful lessons in paying attention to their boards and shareholders. One who clearly understands who works for whom is Kenneth A. Macke of Dayton Hudson. Cited by *Business Week*, *Fortune*, and in academic studies as a model of corporate governance, the Minneapolis retailer has nevertheless just recovered from a disastrous 1992: earnings tumbled after floods in Chicago closed its largest store, Marshall Field, for more than a week and the recession hurt many others.

Reported *Business Week*: "Such a deluge of bad news would make some executives fear for their jobs. Not Kenneth A. Macke. Because of a practice almost unique in corporate America, Dayton's chairman and CEO knows precisely where he stands with his board. Each year Dayton's directors give him a thorough performance review—just like the one every other employee gets. While this year's was tough, he says, it helped him focus on what he could do better, such as lowering expenses and boosting market share. 'You need the support of the board in bad years,' explains Macke. At all too many companies, the CEO wields most of the power in the boardroom. He sets the agenda. At Dayton, directors have access to any of [Macke's] management team. Twelve out of 14 directors are outsiders."

How independent is the Dayton Hudson board? In the bad year, the board withheld Macke's bonus, which had been $600,000 the year before. Big institutional investors supported Macke and the company even in the recent times of trouble because of the CEO's governance philosophy.

From the day the company went public in 1960, only the CEO and chief operating officer were allowed to be insider board mem-

Despite a dismal 1992 for Dayton Hudson, institutional investors praised chief executive Kenneth Macke for the independence of his board.

◆

bers. The 12 outside directors make up the executive committee, and one is the board's vice-chairman, who deals directly with Macke. Directors are limited to a 12-year term and must step down if their jobs change. They give Macke his head in running the company but rigorously spin what Jay Lorsch of Harvard calls the board's "wheel of supervision."

In large companies, CEOs are catching on. The chief executives of Lockheed and Texaco, for instance, show a list of board candidates to institutional investors, allowing them a say in who is picked. Time Warner and others invite recommendations for board seats from shareholder groups. After Time Warner CEO Gerald M. Levin heard complaints from Calpers, he assigned two directors to meet with the shareholder group. He also cut back the company's compliant 21-member board to 15 by dropping all but two management directors and bringing in four outsiders.

These days, the boss must be more like a politician running for office than a ruling potentate. And just like a politician, he must court his keepers. Media consultants advise him. Public-relations executives spin for him. Crisis teams rehearse him for unexpected disasters. Speechwriters and coaches prepare him for public appearances. Lobbyists and lawyers represent him in state and federal governments.

But no constituency must be wooed as assiduously as his board.

The key to good board relations is information. Surprises are the fastest route to CEO mortality. J. Peter Grace, 47-year veteran CEO of W.R. Grace, the company founded by his family, put it well: "No secrets and no fooling around." The curmudgeonly Grace, who sits on half a dozen boards, added, "If you give any director the slightest feeling that you're not telling the whole story, that's when trouble starts."

Director Rawleigh Warner underscored the point: "The CEO never, ever, should surprise the board. That makes outside directors mad. 'Why didn't you tell us? At the last meeting you said this. Now you say this. Why the change?'"

But shouldn't a CEO express realistic optimism? "That's fine, so long as things are going well," answered Warner. "But if the CEO told the board six months ago he didn't see a cloud on the horizon and all of a sudden the company's got a substantial loss, not from some outside force but because of operations, then you have to say to yourself, *I can no longer take his word.*"

So what's the best formula?

"There is no magic formula for empowering directors," concluded Sarah A. B. Teslik, executive director of the Council of Institutional Investors, "but waiting for a cataclysm to force the board's hand is clearly the worst formula of all."

Still, in the troubled new environment of corporate governance, there is virtual unanimity on how a prudent CEO can avoid the pratfalls of many of his contemporaries—if his managing and other skills are up to snuff. From successful CEOs, advisers, directors, academics, lawyers, and others, the consensus is: Consider your relationship with the board (and shareholders) in good times rather than bad. And share doubts and problems as well as hopes and plans. It's safer that way. "I wasn't a bit eager to get caught out on a limb by myself," recalled former Pfizer CEO Ed Pratt. "Right at the start, I told my board members, 'You're going to be out there with me.'"

Sharing the heat is after all part of the board's responsibility—and may even give the board the best view of your strengths. "I can't think of anything that would show your confidence more than to let the board review you the way they're supposed to," said board adviser Ira Millstein. "The best CEOs I know go to their boards and say, What do you want? Do whatever you want. Ask whatever you want. Have the committees you want. I want to be criticized. I want you to look at me. Why? Because I need the board to be my partner. They can't be my partner and part of the solution if I don't give them everything they need to do their work."

President Clinton remembers that before his wife joined the campaign that landed him in the White House, she was on the Wal-Mart board: "I was always fascinated by the way those executives would sit around and have their meetings and take some issues and just talk it through to death and get every angle of it."

Added Hillary Rodham Clinton: "And not in a hierarchical way—in a team approach, where people were just as likely to say to Sam Walton, 'I think that's the craziest idea I ever heard,' as they were to say, 'Gee, I agree with you, Sam.'"

If the company should hit an iceberg as Exxon did with its Valdez oil spill, or NBC with its faked GM truck crash episode, or Union Carbide with its Bhopal, India, gas leak, tell the directors before they hear the news elsewhere, or at least as soon as you hear about it yourself. Don't automatically pooh-pooh the damage (Exxon), immediately get combative (NBC), or fumble around (Union Carbide) until you really know what you're talking about.

And don't blame your press agent if the company gets in trouble, confusing bad public relations with bad behavior. After finally conceding NBC had staged the truck crash, CEO Robert Wright made the mistake of telling the press, "The company's health is actually pretty good. It's the public relations that haven't been good." Wright survived, but the NBC News president under him didn't, nor did NBC News' reputation.

If you're lucky, some board members will come right out and tell you just what they expect. "I'm now on a lot of boards," said Ed Pratt, "and when a new CEO comes along, the first thing I tell him is, 'Don't think you're doing something wrong if the board ever second-guesses you. What the hell good are they for you if they're just patsies?' It's a question of confidence. You've got to be self-confident without being arrogant."

Steadily declining earnings, falling or just static stock prices, and complaints from institutional shareholders often lead to a crisis that forces a board to act. But most directors agree that surprises are the biggest single cause of board action against a CEO. Walter B. Wriston, the crusty former CEO of Citicorp, put it bluntly: "We all agreed that the [unnamed] fellow had to go. You can't have somebody tell you X when it's really Y."

To Drew Lewis, CEO of Union Pacific, if a board opposes or has reservations about a CEO's plans, the course is clear: "You back off. Not because you're afraid of the board, but because you have people on the board who are as capable or more capable than you are, and you have to listen."

"I really don't believe it's my job to 'run' this company," Avis CEO Joseph V. Vittoria said. "It's my responsibility to communicate with the people who run this company."

Some CEOs get only one chance to find this out. Kenneth H. Olsen, the founder and longtime CEO of Digital Equipment, astonished his seven-member board with unexpected losses of close to $3 billion. Accustomed to record-breaking profits from the $14-billion-a-year computer company, the board, which included three of the chairman's close friends, forced his resignation. "I was fired," the CEO bitterly told his staff.

Most directors are willing to go along when there's bad news if it doesn't come as a shock or if the CEO seems to have a plan to deal with the problem. Said Joan Ganz Cooney, a longtime director on several boards and founder of the Children's Television Workshop: "Once the board understands the downside and the upside, it's still going to vote with you. The board gets contentious or negative or worried when they think the downside is being withheld or glossed over, and the company could be seriously hurt."

IN SELECTING THE WORLD CHAMPION MIDSIZE JET, THE JUDGES HAVE REACHED A SPLIT DECISION.

Many owners say the Citation VI is the perfect midsize business jet. No other aircraft offers more speed and more stand-up cabin space for less money. Many other owners say the Citation VII is the world's best midsize jet. It's just as spacious as the VI, but it's even more powerful, more versatile, and more technically advanced.

So, is the ideal midsize jet the Citation VI or the Citation VII? Judging by the popularity of the two, we'd say the answer is "yes."

THE SENSIBLE CITATIONS

Cessna
A Textron Company

Bad news puts the board on alert. "The CEO may tell you, 'I think we have to continue this course,'" said lawyer and Equitable director Arthur Liman. "So you give him a warning. You say, 'We understand that. We're very uncomfortable, but would you watch it carefully?' You can agree to disagree. But if that happens often enough, then you reach a point where the CEO and the inside directors are asked to leave the room."

The perilous line you walk with your board requires careful self-assessment. Donald S. Perkins, former CEO of Jewel Companies, the midwestern grocery distributor, has proposed a governance checklist for CEOs, a pocket guide to measure CEO-board relations. Said Perkins, a mellow governance philosopher who sits on 10 boards and has turned down 80 more, "A perfect CEO should be able to answer yes to these 10 questions":
• If you had a choice, would you even have a board? Would it include the same directors you have now?
• Is your board strong enough to say no to you?
• If you were hit by a truck, is your board informed enough to pick your successor?
• Do you and your officers listen more than talk to your board?
• Have you taught the directors enough about the company and industry so they can be thoughtful critics of your strategy?
• Do your directors know how to evaluate your performance?
• Are your compensation, nominating, and audit committees independent?
• Do you seek board advice and counsel before making important decisions?
• Do you keep your board informed about significant differences of opinion within your management team?
• Would an outside observer of a board meeting conclude that you are a corporate employee performing under the independent oversight of your board?
Whether or not you endorse Perkins's test, you may still protest, "But *I* want to run my company. And not by committee, with my executives, a board, shareholders, the press, or others second-guessing me all the time. American industry was built by spirited individuals, entrepreneurs with a vision, not by boards or shareholder advisers. Look at Edwin H. Land, the genius who founded Polaroid and said, 'The essence of business leadership

is to be able to turn your back on the demands of the financial world.'"

The answer: You're probably not a genius. Anyway, Land retired as CEO in 1980, another era. Go ahead and run your company, but let the board run itself. You don't own the company. You were just put there to lead it, subject to a board that has to answer to its conscience and to the shareholders.

Still, some CEOs decide to dig in their heels despite board rumblings. "Quite often," said Joan Ganz Cooney, "the CEO sort of juts his chin out. 'If you don't go along with me, I'm history.' And the board gets scared—so they do it. It may work. But just as often it doesn't."

The street of governance is not one way. Although they may not remind you of this, directors must be rigorous about their job for you to be exemplary in yours. James D. Woods, chairman and CEO of Baker Hughes, a Houston-based manufacturer of drilling equipment with 1992 sales of $2.5 billion, pushes the issue with his board. He demands an annual formal evaluation of board members, like a year-end report card. Directors are anonymously rated on a scale of one to 10 by fellow board members in 15 categories of performance and contribution. If they repeatedly fall below the 7.5 norm, they may be asked to leave. And in turn, the board evaluates Woods. "Corporate America has more often based board membership on business contacts and social acquaintances with a CEO or other board members," said Woods, "than on a process that objectively attempts to represent the interests of the stockholders."

At least once annually the outside directors ought to meet without you or other company executives present. After all, the board's most important role is to review and judge you, just as you do with your employees. That way, low ratings won't blindside you or the board.

Manville Company, based in Denver, is proof that having the right directors can save your job or even your company. Once the largest U.S. producer of asbestos, Manville became the pariah of American industry when, in the late '70s, scientists discovered that inhaled asbestos could cause lung cancer and other diseases. Warning labels on the company's products did not prevent thousands of lawsuits. The board forced management to declare protective bankruptcy in 1982 and set up a court-supervised trust to settle the medical claims. In 1989 the company emerged from bankruptcy and began returning a profit. W. Thomas Stephens, who has been with Manville for 30 years, nine as CEO, described how his company survived: "The board appointed a special committee of outside directors to study the situation. [They] put everyone on a level playing field: present health claimant, bank creditor, and future health claimant." The result was an innovative plan that separates the reorganized company from future asbestos liability while independent trusts to which the company contributes settle the claims.

"As directors we have to anticipate events," said Stephens. "A board with the right kind of directors can mean the difference between surviving into prosperity or joining the ranks of the forgotten, or worse, the banished."

So how does the CEO find the right directors? Nominating committees should play the major role in recruiting new directors and forming board committees. They need your advice and consent, but not your iron thumb. "If the CEO ever gets himself in a position where he proposes somebody for the board who's unacceptable to the others," Arthur Liman warned, "it results in a vote of no confidence. The CEO cannot afford a vote like that. If you're a good CEO, you have to have consensus."

"Good" CEOs are now making clear to prospective directors that they must be prepared to devote as much time to their work as diligence requires. Directors who do are not overpaid. Some CEOs also encourage directors to hold substantial amounts of stock—just as the CEO should—to better appreciate the shareholders' perspective.

The new interest in boards and shareholders and their treatment by management is not the passing fad of a stressed economy. No one—well, only six percent of CEOs surveyed in 1992—believes that. Even if you are among that dogged minority, it's safer to act as if enlightened corporate governance is here to stay—if you hope to stay.

Although only 10 percent of CEOs have been fired or retired prematurely in the past five years, CEOs plainly are being forced out in increasing numbers. Their golden parachutes waft on the breezes of euphemisms such as "retiring to spend more time with his family" or "pursuing other interests." They all mean one word: fired. As Winston Churchill wrote, "When you have to kill a man, it costs nothing to be polite."

Your board is learning the polite but formidable touch. The directors, in tandem with the marketplace, are pressing you harder—in part because they too have become a vulnerable bunch.

SCHEDULE A BUSINESS MEETING
NEXT DOOR TO THE SOUND BARRIER.

Inside, it is an elegant conference room. Quiet. Abundantly spacious. Beautifully appointed. With soft leather recliners, individual television monitors, and a private dressing room.

Outside, it is slicing through the sky at more than 870 feet per second. Mach .90. One-tenth of a point below the speed of sound.

The remarkable new Citation X. Reservations will be accepted soon for demonstration flights in 1995. And they'll be going fast.

THE SENSIBLE CITATIONS

Cessna
A Textron Company

Chapter Six

DIRECTORS:
A WAKE-UP CALL

Most CEOs serve on the boards of other companies. As a result, a wise CEO needs to know how to be a successful director as well as how to deal with directors on his own board. The symbiosis can be helpful or troublesome, depending on how each relationship is undertaken and managed.

Experienced if cynical CEOs could once joke that "directors are like firemen. They sit around doing very little until there's a fire alarm, and then they spring into action." No longer. Alarm bells have been ringing in too many American companies. CEOs and directors have to face that new reality.

If lounging around the boardroom firehouse is your métier, all current advice warns you *not* to become a director of a large public company. With a rising tide of shareholders seeking more response from management through their board representatives, directors are attacked by shareholders and the media too often for them to play a passive role.

A major directorship takes work—by most estimates a minimum of three or four weeks a year. Directors are the private-sector governors of corporations. Unlike elected public officials, however, if you're a director, the CEO and the rest of the board can remove you without any elaborate elections or impeachment rules. Of course, you can also be sued or in rare instances turned out by your constituents, the shareholders. Not so rarely, fellow directors can dump you when your term is up. Federal regulators can lean on you and punish you for inattention. The media can crucify you.

None of this is likely, but all of it is possible and indeed has happened to more than a few somnolent board members. It is avoidable if you take some simple precautions and do your work seriously. Boards of directors are no longer honorary associations of friendly businessmen. They have become the court of first resort if things turn sour. If you are not prepared to be an active, inquiring judge, don't join a board.

For a CEO in office, joining two or at most three other boards can be a broadening experience. For retired CEOs or so-called professional directors, who serve on many boards as their principal occupation, it can be rewarding in other ways. In large companies, directors' fees range from $40,000 to $90,000 a year, with $1,000 or $2,000 more for each committee meeting. Pay is just the beginning. Most big companies provide life, medical, accident, and liability insurance, a pension, company-matched charitable contributions, and gifts of stock or options that can be worth $250,000 or more.

The material rewards can be seductive, turning some directors into management's toadies rather than active naysayers when necessary. Said a spokeswoman from the Investor Responsibility Research Center, "Many shareholders express doubts that a director on eight or 10 boards, no matter how talented and how well intentioned, can spend the time and thought that's needed."

Before you join a board with all its perks, pleasures, and rewards, make sure you know a lot about the company. Do your homework by reading past proxy statements, analysts' reports, 10Ks, press clippings, and any other pertinent material. It may seem easy to sign on because your good friend Joe, the CEO, has invited you. But old friend or not, make sure that he and you understand your first duty is monitoring his performance, maybe even firing him. In his 1992 article "The Naked Emperors" in *Across the Board* magazine, management consultant Arnold Brown points out that boards must be able to give corporate managers the honest but unwelcome news, in the private confines of the boardroom, that "You don't have any clothes on."

In the past, board service was different. *The Economist* described most directors of public companies as "supine wielders of the rubber stamp." No wonder. Directors were—and many still are—enveloped in largess from and camaraderie with the CEOs they were supposed to direct. They met and worked in humidors of aged power, shielded from the shareholders and the prying public. Infrequent and convivial meetings of the old boys were held in some of the most luxuriously appointed and seldom-used rooms in the world.

What voting took place in the masculine all-white hideouts was almost inevitably unanimous. Board minutes were often so circumspect they revealed nothing. Everyone appeared to say collectively what only a few may have believed individually. A *New Yorker* cartoon reprinted in a 1989 issue of *Business Week* depicted a flock of ostriches dressed in business suits sitting around a board table. It aptly captured the retreat from reality.

Gerard R. Roche, chairman of the search firm Heidrick & Struggles, described the bonhomie that in many cases continues: "There's almost an implicit contract when an individual brings in a board member. They're saying, 'You're a friend of mine, and we don't want any trouble. If there's a problem, we'll handle it between us.'"

The CEO, who in almost every case was also the chairman, picked the board from his (there were few *hers*) circle of like-minded friends. Informal encounters took place in country clubs and shooting blinds, after church, at friendly dinners, and in resorts in the sun or snow. They were as cementing as the meetings around the board table. In large firms, company jets (with no telltale corporate insignia) whisked directors to Augusta, Georgia, for the annual Masters golf tournament, the Super and Rose bowls, or such male bastions as the Bohemian Grove or the Conquistadors del Cielo. The well-fed, well-paid, or well-born business establishment ruled.

But early warning blips began to show up on the radar screen.

In the 1960s and '70s, passive directors got a stark comeuppance. Scandals over illegal political contributions, insider trading, board inattentiveness, overseas bribes, and other shenani-

"The motion has been made and seconded that we stick our heads in the sand."

gans rocked companies such as Texas Gulf Sulphur, Penn Central, and Equity Funding. By 1985 courts began to rule that directors who did not apply "a critical eye" to companies could be held accountable. Both the SEC and the New York Stock Exchange took notice by demanding that boards add more independent outside directors to audit the practices and ethics of the corporations.

"That was the beginning of the modern, independent director having any significant role in corporate affairs—the negative role of a policeman," said corporate lawyer Martin Lipton. "And then, in the late '70s and '80s, came the one magnificent fallout of the takeover era. It forced independent directors to decide whether to take or reject offers and how to create long-range plans and defenses against raiders. The outside independent director began to have a very important role."

If not everywhere, in many boardrooms the change is becoming palpable, even though remnants of the old system abound. No CEO can afford to ignore what's new by relying on what was.

On boards in 1993, the balance of inside and outside directors has shifted from 50-50 to at least 75 percent who are not in the company and are called independent directors. Of the 100 largest companies, 96 now have a majority of outside directors, a far cry from the early '70s when many companies—Pfizer, Exxon, Dow Chemical—had few if any outside directors. Inside directors are management; they can hardly be expected objectively to evaluate their own performance.

At first, after the shock of the 1980s, if public companies thrived, few investors cared about the boards. But the '90s recession and foreign competition stalled the economy, and some of the largest public companies fell far behind, wallowing in their past glory. A barrage of criticism hit CEOs and their obliging boards.

Under the bold headline "Directors Wake Up!," a June 1992 issue of *Fortune* proclaimed that "big investors in stocks of chronically awful companies are finally mad as hell and not going to take it anymore. And they've decided whose neck is on the line." The boardroom culture is changing, the article affirmed, quoting one executive's characterization: "A good director is a 'pain in the ass'—a guy who recognizes that he's not working to be the friend of the CEO but to do what's right for the owners."

After joining the board of a big, starchy midwestern company, one prominent director, a former high government official, objected to the ethics and legality of a move urged by the CEO. The company lawyer answered, "People like you from New York…" Said the new director: "You have five seconds to apologize or I leave." He got his apology, and the CEO dropped the questionable proposal.

Delaware chancellor William T. Allen, the leading arbiter of business disputes in the U.S., pointed out the new obligations directors bear. "The waters of corporate governance have been stirred, and they will not be stilled," he said in 1992. "The evolution of a global market and the growth of institutional investors are dynamic [forces]. They will, they are now pushing [for] greater efficiency and accountability." It is the board that will lead the public to adjust to this new reality, he continued. "The most elementary and important adaptation is a redefinition in the minds of those men and women who serve on corporate boards of [their] legal and social requirements."

How much have boards changed in accepting these new responsibilities? The evidence is mixed. But the combination of vastly increased board and shareholder activism reported here suggests that the changes are more than Panglossian hopes.

OF ALL THE SOPHISTICATED TOOLS USED TO BUILD CITATION BUSINESS JETS, THIS ONE IS THE MOST IMPORTANT.

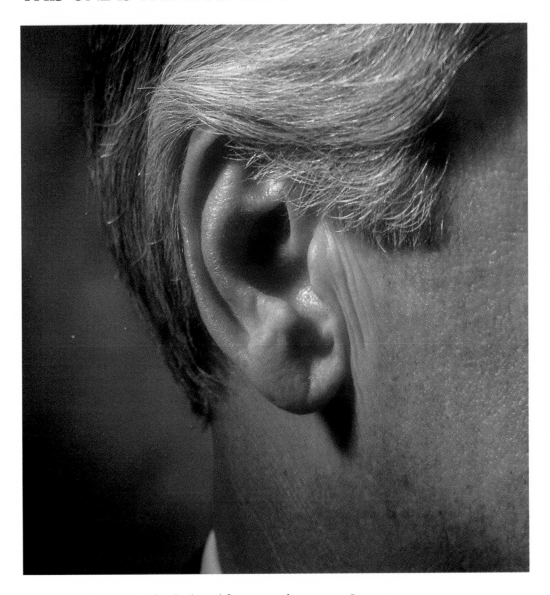

Among the many individuals and forums we listen to at Cessna is an independent group of pilots and maintenance experts we call our Advisory Council. On the new Citation X they said, "Give us a 320-kt climb speed, wider baggage door and easy avionics access." So we did. Along with hundreds of other things to make our Citations the best they can possibly be for the people who use them. It's really not very complicated how we know precisely what Citation operators want and need in their aircraft. We simply ask them.

THE SENSIBLE CITATIONS

Cessna
A Textron Company

"When I started it was not quite honorific but close. It's very different now," said Joan Ganz Cooney, a corporate director for almost 20 years. "There are pressures you feel all the time—from the shareholders, the regulators, public opinion, and the media. The press was once very weak on business. Then suddenly, because of the '80s, the whole world got fascinated. Active younger CEOs are coming on boards who are not there because they're friends of the chairman. Boards are firing CEOs now."

And shareholders are ousting directors. Said Ira Millstein, "If the board pays no attention to why the company isn't doing well or doesn't care to do anything about it, shareholders have every right to try to get rid of the board. Boards are increasingly getting the notion that they can be replaced, that they're not in concrete, that just because they got selected by the CEO, it's not lifetime employment. Boards are much more sensitive to the fact that large shareholders are out there who can act. If the board knows that a significant number of shareholders might be able to move on them, the board is going to be responsible."

Beverly Sills Greenough, the celebrated onetime opera star who seems to have an affinity for the boards of troubled corporations—Macy's, AmEx, Time Warner—recalls more pleasant times. When she started in 1983, she says, meetings were easy. "There were never decisions or votes that I went home and worried about. At Macy's, in the old days, we had a board discussion about the floors in the elevators where some of the women were getting their heels caught, and another about putting a new air conditioner in the furniture section of Bamberger's. It's totally different now. Companies are very wary of having an uninformed board. The boys' club has broken up. There's too much risk."

George Anders, financial writer and author of *Merchants of Debt*, characterizes the change: "The barbarians of the '80s have not retreated. Instead many have simply moved into the boardroom. In the 1980s the dominant issues were financial." Now they are managerial. Chicago lawyer Elmer W. Johnson, a former GM executive vice-president, warned an applauding audience at the 1990 convention of the National Association of Corporate Directors: "Most boards would be well advised to take a careful look at their composition and culture, their practices and procedures, and to prepare for the '90s and the intense new focus on corporate governance."

Harvard professor Jay W. Lorsch still finds many boards largely dysfunctional. According to his study of governance issues, *Pawns and Potentates*, written with Elizabeth MacIver, directors remain inbred, confused about their role, mixed up about where their loyalties lie, and too often unquestioning until the company is in a crisis. His hope is that directors will become "more like the corporate potentates the law intends them to be than the management pawns they have too often been in the past."

One gradual change is the representation of minorities. Woe to the big company that has neither a woman nor a black on its board. Graef Crystal, the corporate compensation expert, only half jokes that CEOs now try to fill their boards with "10 friends of the management, a woman, and a black." But blacks still represent less than three percent of the directors on the boards of the 1,000 biggest U.S. companies. Women have fared better, although they are still on only one in 20 public-company boards.

Marian Heiskell, an owner of *The New York Times* and the first woman on the boards of Ford, Merck, and Consolidated Edison, tells of joining the Ford board in 1975, when she was in her mid-fifties: "Henry Ford II at first screamed and hollered like a banshee. He wasn't about to have a woman on the board. It'll spoil the club. But he changed his mind and finally invited me on.

"When I arrived for my first board meeting, they had a special bedroom fixed up for me, near the boardroom like all the other directors. But—can you imagine?—they brought in Tampex, Kotex, a few little perfume bottles, and a hair dryer. Then they gave me a gym suit. I asked, Why do you want me to come to the gym? They said, Because we want you to let the other female executives know that the gym is for them also. I said, But you don't have any female executives. They got one, finally, but she never came to the gym."

Despite all the evidence of an awakening by board directors, some are still drowsing. What hazard do they run?

"Liability" is the resounding answer. "You can be sued and held responsible," said many directors in chorus. Lawsuits against directors abound. The average claim since 1990 is $3 million;

the average defense costs $600,000. For directors such suits can take many days and much energy, but the direct financial risk is negligible.

All large public companies take out multimillion-dollar liability insurance for their directors, known as "D&O" policies—directors' and officers' insurance. Depending on the size of the company, some policies insure directors for $200 million, and the company pays the escalating premiums. Cases where directors of public companies (excluding financial service companies) have personally paid any judgment are rare. Everyone agrees the more potent liability is public embarrassment.

It's a different story if you're the director of a commercial bank, an insurance company, or other financial service company. There the liability can be real. Said John D. Hawke Jr., chairman of Arnold & Porter in Washington, D.C., and a leading banking lawyer, "The banking regulators view the board as the last line of defense for the federal interest. The fundamental difference between a financial board and a nonfinancial one is the extent to which regulators deal directly with directors and try to impose a responsibility on them."

If the regulators find fault with the bank, they may call the directors together and present them with draft remedies. Regulators can also ask directors to sign a remedial agreement. If the violations are not cleared up, the regulators may assess the directors for the amount not covered by D&O insurance.

In the savings and loan scandals, the FDIC sued one out of 30 S&L directors. "When a bank fails," said Hawke, "the FDIC steps in as the receiver. It stands in the shoes of the institution. It has the right to assert any claims that the corporation could have asserted. So that if the directors were arguably negligent, the FDIC will sue them. In a number of cases, directors have paid substantial amounts beyond what's covered by insurance." For example, in 1993 directors of the failed First Republic Bank of Dallas paid $22 million out of their own pockets.

Nevertheless, lawyer Ira Millstein thinks that a diligent director need have no more apprehension about serving on a financial board than on a nonfinancial one. "Sure, banks are a different environment," he said, "but if you read, do your homework, are reasonably diligent, and use your head, the chances of being liable are very remote. You don't need to be a rocket scientist to be a board member. All you have to do is be attentive, reasonably intelligent, and keep your eyes open."

Director Rawleigh Warner agreed. "You wouldn't go on a board unless you were thoroughly satisfied that the D&O insurance was adequate. There's no major personal liability except for criminal malfeasance. What really concerns you is looking like a fool and having your name tarnished as somebody who's been duped by the management. You're supposed to be involved. Of course, you've got to be careful about the kind of company you go into."

Whether you are a rocket scientist or not, sitting on a major board is no longer a cakewalk. "What directors can do best," said Arthur Liman, "apart from moments of crisis like removing the CEO, is to raise questions, to challenge the premises of corporate policies, and to ask for the answers. They therefore impose a discipline on management." The best directors also know when to stop asking questions. They recognize the difference between being a collaborator or a collaborationist. The former can be a usefully constructive critic; the latter is a traitor to principle.

Said Beverly Sills Greenough: "Henry Kissinger and I sit together at the board table of American Express. The discussion is heavily financial. Often he'll say to me or I to him, 'What does that mean?' I'll say, 'Henry, we have to ask,' so we stop and ask."

The worst director is one who carries on at the board meeting and is never heard from in between. Said a prominent CEO and board adviser, "The director ought to let the CEO know what's on his mind and not wait for the board meeting. That can be the worst possible time to have a discussion; it tends to become confrontational or people become defensive and you pull your punches. There's no reason why a director can't go to a CEO and say, 'I'd like to come up and see you. I'm very concerned about the way this company is operating.'"

Experienced directors insist on getting any necessary information, including, in rare cases, information about the health or personal habits of a CEO. The SEC disclosure requirements don't strictly cover such matters, but they could affect the company's future. Compassion is a necessity; so is realism.

In their paper "A Modest Proposal for Improving Corporate Governance," Martin Lipton and Jay Lorsch suggest that directors hold strategy sessions each year, "not in the Bahamas or the

Scotland golf courses but at company headquarters with the division heads, the plant managers, and others so that the directors have the opportunity for knowledge in depth of the strategic issues involved in approving management's goals."

All agree that no matter how diligent directors are, they will never know enough—nor should they in their part-time duties—to function as operating executives. But if an activity becomes a public *cause célèbre*, explanations are in order. Directors bear responsibility for the conduct of a company as well as its bottom line. In its 1993 ranking of most admired American corporations, *Fortune* observed that if hard numbers account for half of a company's reputation, the other half can be far more ephemeral. Wise management, high-quality products and services, and the ability to attract talented employees are critical to reputation.

Getting acquainted with some of the managers and employees, as well as visiting the sites of the company's operations, is also useful. (If the CEO or senior managers balk, directors ought to do more than wonder why.) Directors can learn a lot away from the bubble of the boardroom.

As soundproof as directors may feel the boardroom is, it has glass windows. Everybody, especially the press, is asking questions. Few secrets are secure. These days CEOs and directors have to be as ready as government officials to justify their actions.

Chancellor Allen explained the necessity: "I understand that boards should generally be cooperative, collegial organs. [But] it is [not] efficient to purchase collegiality at the price of passivity. A director's role [is] imbued with some elements of a public or civic responsibility. I see the men and women who accept this responsibility as performing a service to the whole community, to the nation. In doing so there is honor. But in playing the comfortable role of genial adviser there is little honor; there may, ultimately, be dishonor. The notion of honor and an unenforceable but nonetheless real public duty may strike you as quaint, as a ghost of an earlier age. But I hold to another hope: that we have not forgotten the claims that duty can legitimately make upon us, for the benefit of strangers."

Those "strangers" are not only the American investors but the American people as well.

CESSNA HAS INVESTED A QUARTER-BILLION DOLLARS TO KEEP CITATION OPERATORS IN THEIR PLACE.

A Citation's place is in the sky. That's why every Citation is supported by the largest single-product network of any business jet in the world. Today, eight company-owned Citation Service Centers are dedicated entirely to Citations. And authorized Service Stations are located around the globe. It's a quarter-billion-dollar investment.

We figure the more we spend on the Citation service network, the less time Citation owners will spend on the ground.

THE SENSIBLE CITATIONS

Cessna
A Textron Company

Chapter Seven

A COMMON SENSE EVOLUTION

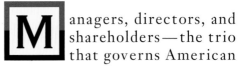anagers, directors, and shareholders—the trio that governs American business—have each had a different role in the economy. Before the 1980s managers ran companies, and boards mostly followed management's lead. Shareholders harvested their profits or, if disappointed, planted their money in the soil of another company.

After the high-calorie '80s, lean times—brought on by a witches' brew of debt, foreign competition, and recession—changed the '90s corporate diet. Boards held managers more accountable. Directors, in turn, felt the new activism of giant shareholder groups, which had been freed to band together by the SEC.

The uproar affected workers as well. In the "leaning and meaning" of American corporations, management eliminated millions of jobs. Wall Street and others cheered when dinosaur companies awakened to modern reality.

It could be argued that the dereliction of many CEOs, boards, and shareholder-owners made the massive bloodletting a harsh necessity. Had they been more alert, a less painful evolution could have eased the devastation in the nameless ranks of many companies. "Downsizing," it was euphemistically called. Some labeled it "dumbsizing."

"Business annals are strewn with the wreckage of companies that cut their way into ruin," a prominent Minneapolis banker pointed out. Added IBM lawyer Richard M. Goldman: "Innovation and marketing have to replace downsizing and restructuring. Downsizing is not a solution. It's a cover-up of earlier mismanagement. Incumbent executives resort to downsizing to cover up their mistakes, and new executives use it to cover up the mistakes of the directors who hired them."

GM's new CEO, Jack Smith, got to the point in his grim 1993 letter to shareholders: "GM is hard-pressed to ask for loyalty and commitment from its employees" as it lays off thousands of its own. Secretary of Labor Robert B. Reich, a specialist in workplace attitudes, underscores the problem: "Unless people feel they will be valued over the long term, they may be more reluctant to go the extra mile, to think a little harder, to contribute in the same way."

The Founders designed the American democratic political system to be untidy. They gave no one person or group absolute power. Instead, they fashioned an experiment—rooted in rights— that their successors would refine in waves of change. With all its glitches and shortfalls, the system is the world's most successful model of democracy. It has survived the Civil War, the Great Depression, cold and hot wars, and the transforming revolutions of the '60s, '70s, and '80s.

The American business enterprise system is different. It has no Founders and—most important—no Constitution or Supreme Court. But it too, with all its glitches and shortfalls, is still the envy of much of the world. Its ad hoc rules, accompanied by state and federal regulation, encourage individuals and groups to figure out patterns of achievement themselves. Its most important regulator is not the ballot box but the marketplace.

America's political and business systems achieve democracy by indirection—through representatives. Although participatory political democracy and the desire for a more democratic role in business are vastly different, they bear striking similarities.

In the '90s, the electorate of the business system—the shareholders—began to demand more accountability from the boards in companies where the system was failing.

Their desire was less to take over than to be more involved. Their motives were as impure and as mixed as those of the national political electorate. From their special-interest pedestals, they often sent confusing signals. Some sought instant gratification; others wanted only future security. Still others behaved like George Steinbrenners, ready to fire the manager and the front office at the first sign their team was losing.

True, many managers of companies and their boards needed the discipline. Too many had plainly arrogated excessive authority, which results could not justify. Too often they stuck to their old plans even when the marketplace and shareholders rejected them. They seemed to forget the meaning of a public company, that their public, the shareholders, had a right to be heard.

Margaret Thatcher, Britain's Iron Lady, once observed, "The main cause of problems is solutions." Corporate governance offers no solutions, only evolutions.

At the outset of this inquiry, I expected to find bruising discord among CEOs, directors, and shareholders over how best to respond to their new environment. Name-calling, finger-pointing, and acrimony mark most periods of upheaval. Surprisingly, more consensus than clash emerged.

It was as if the three had participated in successful group therapy, each emerging with a new set of good intentions on how to live together more comfortably. There were, of course, marginal dissents, but mostly of the kind that the justices of the Supreme Court file in their concurring opinions even when they reach a unanimous decision.

This landmark dispute over who's in charge of American companies involves common sense rather than law. Neither Karl Marx nor Adam Smith could ever have predicted this new stage of capitalism. It might not last. But for now most of the leaders of the system know that their governing relationship needs to be dependent rather than hostile and standoffish. Certainly each of the three groups had to make readjustments. Almost in one voice they agreed on what the most critical of those readjustments were. "There is a yearning out there to rise above partisanship," reported social analyst Daniel Yankelovich. "People are tired of one group of people making points off another." According to George Fisher of Motorola, the three groups acknowledge a need for realignment. "Our financial system is a good system," he said, "and we could make it better. We have a very good base on which to build."

The advice proffered here to CEOs, directors, and shareholders reflects that yearning. It is a distillation of a widespread consensus. Some—especially those who think nothing is wrong—may argue that we should wait for the good old days to return. Satisfying all views runs the risk of banality—Polonius-like advice that all could endorse but few would follow. Yet overwhelmingly, CEOs, directors, and shareholders speak and write similar prescriptions, not for rewriting their common-law constitution but for achieving its true intent. To do so will require many changes, grouped under the rubric "creative tension," in the ways each of the three groups needs to act.

The changes suggested are not draconian. Perhaps that is because the seemingly perplexing question of "Who's in Charge?" requires no solution or blunt answer, only an easement—a modification in attitude, not of rules. As corporate management becomes more responsive to active boards, which in turn more truly represent the interests of longer-term investors, a new balance among all three could be struck. With corporations in better alignment, both private and public sectors can work more effectively on the fundamental economic and societal problems that are tormenting Americans in the '90s.

"Corporate governance needs no government intervention," summarized Ira Millstein, "no regulation, no new laws, but requires simply asking questions of boards of directors in good faith and evaluating the credibility of the board members and their answers. The process itself must certainly lead to an awareness that change is needed and that managers who can't or won't change must be replaced."

Who could honestly say we should not turn—armed with more awareness—to the task of making those readjustments in the way business governs itself?

Insert only two changes in President Bill Clinton's inaugural address to find the "right stuff" for business in the '90s: "There is nothing wrong with American *business* that cannot be cured by what is right with American *business*."

ADDITIONAL COPIES

To order additional copies of *Who's in Charge?*
for friends or colleagues, please write to
The Chief Executive Press, Whittle Books,
333 Main St., Knoxville, Tenn. 37902.
Please include the recipient's name, mailing
address, and, where applicable, title,
company name, and type of business.

For a single copy, please enclose a check
for $13.95, plus $3.50 for shipping and
handling, payable to The Chief Executive
Press. Discounts are available for orders of 10
or more books. If you wish to order by phone,
call 800-284-1956.

Also available, at the same price,
are the previous books from
The Chief Executive Press:
Getting the Job Done by Kenneth L. Adelman,
What Are You Worth? by Graef S. Crystal,
Pressure Points by Robert W. Lear,
and *Found Money* by Al Ehrbar.

Please allow two weeks for delivery.
Tennessee residents must add 8¼ percent sales tax.